A

Trip Through Time

And

The Santa Cruz Mountains

By

Billie J. and Reece C. Jensen

A Trip Through Time and The Santa Cruz Mountains

Second Edition, Revised

Published by the Ghastly Gallimaufry
P.O. Box 2781
Gardnerville, Nevada 89410

Copyright © 1994, 1998 by BILLIE J. and REECE C. JENSEN
First Printing 1994
Second Printing 1998, revised

All rights reserved. No part of this book may be reproduced or transmitted in any form or by any means, electronic or mechanical, including photocopying, recording or by any information storage or retrieval system without written permission from the author, except for the inclusion of brief quotations in a review.

Printed in the U.S.A.

ISBN 1-886278-08-3

Dedication

To the memory of those of our family who have preceded us, and for the nourishment of our first grandchild, Haley Jean, who has just begun to walk the trail, we dedicate this work...

Acknowledgments

The authors wish to thank Frank Adams for the loan and use of family photographs, the biography of Edward F. Adams, and Highland School records.

Also special thanks to William A. Wulf, prominent historian, who supplied many interesting facts and figures relating to the building of the railroad by South Pacific Coast Railway, and the development of the town of Los Gatos, California. The William A. Wulf collection of pictures and historical data, especially on the life and times of George C. Colgrove, to be found at the Los Gatos Public Library, also provided an interesting and reliable source of information.

Also we appreciate the efforts of Lois Knudsen of Database, Gardnerville, Nevada, who helped in our computer conversions, and Mario Duvall, graphic artist of Carson City, Nevada, for his assistance in the preparation of figures.

TABLE OF CONTENTS

CHAPTER		PAGE
	DEDICATION	*iii*
	ACKNOWLEDGEMENTS	*iv*
	TABLE OF FIGURES	*vii*
	DESCRIPTION OF MAP	*ix*
	COMPUTER GENERATED MAP OVERLAY	*x*
	USGS TOPOGRAPHIC MAP OF AREA	*xi*
1	*THE SANTA CRUZ MOUNTAINS*	*1*
2	*LOCAL INDIAN CULTURE*	*3*
3	*ESTABLISHMENT OF THE SPANISH MISSIONS*	*7*
4	*CATTLE RANCHING - A WAY OF LIFE*	*11*
5	*EARLY COOKING*	*13*
6	*SPORTING EVENTS*	*15*
7	*JOHN FREMONT ARRIVES IN CALIFORNIA*	*17*
8	*ARRIVAL OF THE WHITE SETTLERS*	*21*
9	*THE GOLD RUSH YEARS*	*25*
10	*THIEVES AND RUSTLERS*	*27*
11	*EARLY GOVERNMENT IN CALIFORNIA*	*29*
12	*LOS GATOS ("THE CATS")*	*31*
13	*SETTLEMENT OF THE SANTA CRUZ MOUNTAINS*	*33*
14	*MOUNTAIN CHARLEY McKIERNAN*	*37*
15	*VILLA BRANCIFORTE - THE SMUGGLERS' HIDEOUT*	*41*
16	*LUMBER CAMPS IN THE MOUNTAINS*	*43*
17	*EARLY WINE MAKING*	*45*

CHAPTER		PAGE
18	EARLY ROADS AND TOLL GATES	49
19	SPANISH INFLUENCE ON FOOD	53
20	STAGE LINES TO SANTA CRUZ	57
21	TALES OF THE BANDITOS	61
22	STAGE ROBBERS	63
23	ANOTHER CHARLEY OF NOTE	67
24	A RAILROAD COMPANY EMERGES	69
25	RAILROAD CONSTRUCTION	71
26	TRACKS, TRESTLES, AND TUNNELS	77
27	COMPLETION OF THE RAILROAD	81
28	RESORTS AND SPAS ALONG THE RAILROAD	83
29	FAMILY LIFE AT THE TURN OF THE CENTURY	95
30	1893 - A WILD AND WOOLLY WINTER	141
31	HAIR-RAISING RIDES ON THE NARROW GAUGE	143
32	LOS GATOS' CHINA CAMP	145
33	LOS GATOS - "GEM OF THE FOOTHILLS"	147
34	THE GREAT EARTHQUAKE AND FIRE OF 1906	175
	EPILOGUE	183
	RECIPES OF THE ERA	191
	BIBLIOGRAPHY PART 1	217
	BIBLIOGRAPHY PART 2	221
	INDEX	223
	PHOTO ADDENDUM	229-235
	ABOUT THE AUTHORS	236

TABLE OF FIGURES

DESCRIPTION	PAGE
Computer Generated Map Overlay of Key Features	x
Area Map - 1915 USGS Topographic	xi
Flyer and Admission Ticket to Germania Verein Glee Club Picnic	xii
Forbes Mill (Santa Rosa Brand Flour Mill)	24
Hotel de Redwood (Redwood Lodge)	36
Charley and Barbara McKiernan	38
Charley McKiernan	39
The Original "A-Team"	40
The Frederick Hihn Saw Mill	42
The Sears Ranch	48
Concord Stage	56
Early Mountain Settlers, circa 1890	66
Pacific Ocean House, Santa Cruz	68
Locomotive - "The San Mateo"	73
Community of Wrights	74
Community of Laurel	75
The Elusive "Light at the End of the Tunnel" (Laurel to Glenwood)	76
Sketch of Wrights Tunnel	79
Fruit Exchange at Wrights Station	80
Resort Advertisement Signs at Glenwood	82
Alma Railroad Station	84
Wrights Railroad Station	85
Laurel Railroad Station	86
Sketch of La Porte's General Store, Laurel	87
Hotel de Redwood and Surrounding Locale	88
Glenwood Railroad Station	89
Glenwood General Store	90
Glenwood Hotel	91
Glenwood Hotel Postcard	92
Sketch of Hotel Glen Orchy	93
Glenwood Magnetic Springs Resort	94
"My Underwear Budget"	102
Celebration at Burrell School Program	103
Edward F. and Delia Cooper Adams	106
Adams Family on the Porch	107
Adams Family in the Library	108
The Adams' Skyland Ranch - 2 views	109
Adams' Grove	110
Colonel Slaughter's Lagoon	111
Colonel Slaughter's Home	112
A Sunday Outing with Baby	113
Looking Northwest from Crane Ranch	114
A Panoramic View of Three Ranches	115
Will Chamberlain and Daughter	116
Unidentified Civil War-Era Lady	117
Santa Cruz Mountain Farm House	118
Violins at the Saw Mill	119
The Sargent Family on the Veranda	120
Unidentified Gentleman with Pipe	121
Highland School Picture with Katherine Adams	122

DESCRIPTION	PAGE
Flag Raising at Burrell School	123
Sketch of Laurel School	124
Class Picture, circa 1890	125
Croquet at Highland School	126
Skyland Church	127
A "Wedding Chapel"	128
Huntin' or Fishin'?	129
Friendly Poker Game	130
Unidentified Summit Ranch House	131
The Opening Day of the P.P.I.E.	132
Cosmopolitan Hotel	133
Ol' Swimmin' Hole	134
Summit or Highland Road Area	135
The Santa Cruz Mountains	136
Highland School's "Kitchen of the Future"	137
Highland Center "Open-Air-Market"	138
A Horse Named "Mike"	139
Children at Play	140
Northbound Train Looking Into Windy Point	151
Northbound Train Proceeding Towards Los Gatos Station	152
Engine # 15, Los Gatos Station	153
Los Gatos Train Depot	154
Artist Rendition of Main Street, Ad for Adair & Place	155
Photograph of Main Street and North Santa Cruz Ave., circa 1900	156
A View on Main Street, circa 1920	157
Another View on Main Street - Ford Opera House	158
Busy Intersection Showing 3 Modes of Transportation	159
Another View on Main Street from the Bridge Looking West	160
A More Modern View on Main Street	161
Looking East on Main Street	162
North Santa Cruz Avenue, Looking North	163
Newspaper Photograph, circa 1894, Shows Early Los Gatans	164
Newspaper Photograph of Hotel Lyndon Stables	165
Newspaper Photograph West Main Street Showing Early Buildings	166
Newspaper Photograph Showing Los Gatos Agricultural Works	167
Newspaper Photograph Showing First Elementary School	168
Newspaper Photograph Showing First Los Gatos High School	169
Newspaper Photograph Showing Congress Springs	171
San Francisco City Hall after 1906 Earthquake	179
San Francisco Street Scene Showing Earthquake Destruction	180
Stanford University Entrance Showing Earthquake Destruction	181
1st Train to Santa Cruz after Earthquake	187
The Little Town of Alma	188
Commemorative Stamp and Envelope	189
Swift's Silver Leaf Lard Ad	192
E. G. Skinner Ad	196
Hills Brothers Ad	200
Oxnard Undertakers Ad	204
Lyndon Hotel-two views	216
Photo and Memorabilia Addendum	229-235

DESCRIPTION OF HISTORIC MAP

USGS (United States Geological Survey) Topographic Map, circa 1915 (scale 1:62,500) one inch equals one mile. The primary area of interest includes Los Gatos and the pass through the Santa Cruz Mountains leading toward Santa Cruz. The information available in 1915 on the map has generally not been updated on the computer-generated overlay so that the reader may study the way it was more closely to the time the stories in the book took place. In other words, there is no indication of the 20 miles of State Highway 17 (4-lanes), which was completed in 1939 and took most of the twists and turns out of the road lines shown on the overlay. Only the early roads are shown that the animals roamed, the Indians ran, the Franciscans walked, the stage coaches careened over, and the earliest motor driven vehicles took hours to traverse! Some, but not all, of the roads have been traced on the overlay. There are many more that follow the contour lines, which make them difficult to pick out, especially in the Summit and Highland/Skyland areas. Also, some of the road information has been lost in the scanning of the original map.

The same conditions exist for the railroad system (indicted by dashed lines). The overlay is not an accurate plot of the trackbed; however, it represents the best that could be determined under the circumstances where contour lines, creek beds, roads and tracks are, in some instances superimposed, one over the other. Only the two major and longest railroad tunnels are shown. The short bore at Alma is not evident and the other tunnels in the system are west of Glenwood and, hence, off the map.

Only a few of the large Mexican/Spanish Land Grants are shown on the overlay. The Shoquel Augmentation (note the spelling probably like the original map-makers thought it was pronounced), San Augustin, and Rinconada de Los Gatos. For the location of others, see the topographic map directly. At the summit, the San Andreas Fault Line, (not indicated) runs close to or on the Santa Cruz/Santa Clara County Line.

Mountain communities, with their depots and schools and other landmark buildings or noteworthy attractions are indicated. As regards "Beehive", its significance is unknown but it was on Charley McKiernan's property and probably the hub of one of his many pursuits. His cabin residence also served as a toll house for the stage coaches and wagons that, 130 years ago, began to open up this fascinating area.

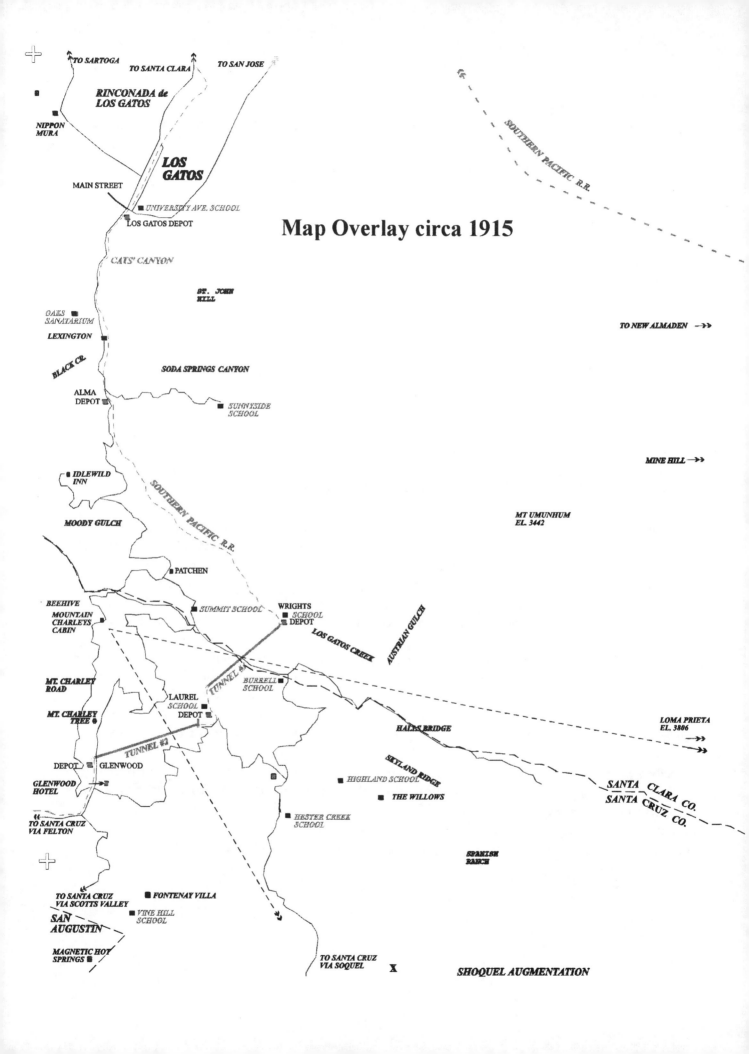

DEPARTMENT OF THE INTERIOR
FRANKLIN K. LANE, SECRETARY
U.S. GEOLOGICAL SURVEY
GEORGE OTIS SMITH, DIRECTOR.

TOPOGRAPHY

Germania Verein Picnic.

GLENWOOD GROVE. **SUNDAY, MAY 21.**

On The South Pacific Coast Railroad.

San Jose, May 8th, 1882.

TO THE MEMBERS OF THE GERMANIA VEREIN:

We beg to lay before you the Programme of this year's Picnic, to be held on Sunday, May 21, 1882, at Glenwood Grove, on the South Pacific Coast Railroad. A lovely spot (far superior to last year's) has been selected, and the greatest precautions have been taken to *Remove all Poison Oak* within 1 1-2 miles circumference.

A SPECIAL TRAIN

Will Leave the Depot on the Alameda at 8:45 A. M. Returning from Glenwood at 6 P. M.
ARRIVAL AT PICNIC GROUNDS AT TEN A. M.

THEN THE POPULAR BARBECUE

Under the management of the irrepressible HY. LUX, ESQ.
The Club furnishes the necessaries for a regular Barbecue: MEATS, of all kinds, BREAD, the Choicest COFFEE, Pure MILK (from Knoche's celebrated dairy) and SUGAR; also Tin Cups and Tin Plates.
BRING ALONG KNIVES AND FORKS.
Lager Beer, Lemonade, Wine and Cigars, at the Bar, at Club Rates.
AFTER THE BARBECUE,

MUSIC, DANCING, AND ALL KINDS OF AMUSEMENTS.

ABOUT INVITATIONS AND TICKETS.

Each member is entitled to invite two gentlemen and their families, and their names have to be handed in to the Committee (in care of Luther, Schroeder & Co.,) on or before MONDAY, May 15th, 1882.

TICKETS: FOR GENTLEMEN, $1.50. LADIES, $1.00. CHILDREN UNDER 12 YEARS, 25 CTS.
Round Trip, Including the Barbecue

All tickets must be taken by THURSDAY Evening, May 18th, 1882, as the Committee has to make its arrangements according to the number of participants. To avoid disappointment, the members are requested to bear this in mind, as NO TICKETS will be sold later. The Expenses are HIGH and the fare LOW, consequently the calculations must be CLOSE.

Tickets will be sold at A. & G. MARTEN'S Dry Goods Store, 311 Santa Clara Street, between First and Second, and INVITATIONS MUST BE PRESENTED in procuring the same.

Committee of Arrangements:

CAPT. WM. STEINBUEHLER, GEORGE C. FRICKE,
HENRY LUX, CHAS. OTTER,
HY. L. SCHEMMEL, G. MARTEN.

MERCURY PRINT.

"All A-board!"
These two mementos courtesy of William A. Wulf.

CHAPTER 1

THE SANTA CRUZ MOUNTAINS

Throughout time, the sentinel-like Santa Cruz Mountains bordering this particular pass have played many roles. They have silently guarded untold riches, offered a haven for wildlife, harbored fugitives, and lured prospectors tempted by any lucrative sounding scheme. They have, so far, even tolerated the slow but inevitable encroaching moves of man up onto their highest peaks and down into their deepest sanctuaries.

As graphically described in Bruce A. MacGregor's SOUTH PACIFIC COAST, "The Santa Cruz Mountains, though not impressively high, are nevertheless ranked among the most rugged." Although a few peaks reach heights of over 3500 feet, basically, he explains, these mountains rise to an average height of only 2500 feet above the Pacific Ocean to the west. Their sheer flanks, steep canyons, high valleys, and strangely unique "double summit", however, hint at some torturous events during their creation.. Traversing them has always been uninviting and fraught with unbelievable hardships.

The northern and southern slopes are a study in contrasts, MacGregor goes on. From the summit, the northern slopes, undulating down toward the beautiful Santa Clara Valley are relatively dry and brushy, dotted here and there with live oak and madrone trees. To the south, the terrain is one of plush green folds, resulting in high crests and hidden mysterious hollows. Here, nourished by the silently creeping ocean fogs, can be found the large open meadows and grasslands surrounded by graceful fir, pine and the majestic, towering redwoods. The mist-loving redwoods, cousins of the giant Sequoia which grow in profusion in the High Sierra, can reach heights of 300 feet or more and only grow in certain areas of the Coastal Range. Sometimes the fog engulfs all but the mountain peaks. From the summit, they appear as lost islands enveloped in a sea of swirling blue-white mist.

Two major sources of water originate on opposite sides of the summit. The headwaters of the San Lorenzo River tumble down toward Monterey Bay, and those of Los Gatos Creek pick up run-off around rugged Cat's canyon as it drops dramatically in the direction of Los Gatos. Eventually, these waters empty into the lower tip of San Francisco Bay.

In normal years, rainfall in the Santa Clara Valley averages about sixteen inches. The Santa Cruz Mountains boast of twice that, or more. Even seventy-five to one hundred inches of seasonal rainfall is not unheard of in some areas where storm clouds tend to back up against the twisted mountain ridges to unleash their fury on whatever is below. Occasionally, seasons of subnormal rainfall and draught conditions tend to push visions of *gully-washers* far from the preoccupied mind but Mother Nature is unpredictable and capricious in her ways.

In addition to the inherent rugged beauty of these mountains, there are many built-in weaknesses and dangers as well. The area is not only at the mercy of torrential winter rains, but also wind-whipped fires during the dry season. About 90% of the mountain soil is susceptible to erosion, sometimes causing major landslides. The famous - or infamous - San Andreas Earthquake Fault traverses the axis of this 55-mile-long range, on or adjacent to its crest. "Measurable fault creep," according to John C. Cummings, in 1968, then-staff member of the U.S. Geological Survey team in Menlo Park, California, "normally very slow over the millennia of geological time, has speeded up to as much as one inch per year during the last decade." Today, it is estimated the fault line in some areas creeps much faster, at a rate of two or more inches per year.

When the fault line becomes more active, there are resulting detectable earthquakes and other subsurface movements which can, and have, resulted in drastic physical changes to the terrain.

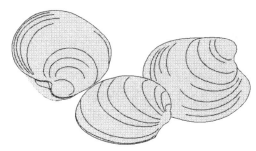

CHAPTER 2

LOCAL INDIAN CULTURE

In many places, the sweeping curves of State Highway 17 today follow the trails of the animals that once roamed in wild profusion throughout the Coastal Range - grizzly bear, mountain lion, bobcat, coyote, wolf and jackal, to name only a few. The animals were formidable but the California Indians, especially those who lived in and about these parts a few hundred years ago, were among the most peace-loving on the North American Continent, according to Ralph J. Roske, author of EVERYMAN'S EDEN. "There were, of course, disagreements and conflicts to some extent, and even a few small-scale wars between individuals and tribes but these skirmishes," according to Roske, "were usually fought for the sake of disputes over productive land areas, revenge of violence, and revenge of witchcraft (in which the California Indians were strong believers)." But, for the most part, the Indians remained in their own provinces, separated from other tribes by their language differences, and by geological barriers of sometimes only a few miles.

According to Betty War Brusa in her book on the Salinan Indians, the Costanoan Indians (a name derived from the word Costenos and given to them by the conquering Spaniards, then changed slightly again to Costanos by the white settlers who followed), were about 7,000 in number. They dwelt in the area that extended from San Francisco south to Soledad, and from the Pacific Ocean east to the Mount Diablo Range. There were three or four good-size villages, of up to perhaps one hundred inhabitants, and numerous smaller communities scattered about the Santa Clara Valley and surrounding mountains.

In the particular area 50 miles south of San Francisco, beyond the lower tip of San Francisco Bay, some Indians preferred the valley floor, while others enjoyed the foothills of the Santa Cruz Mountains - their "Blue Mountains" as they called them. The Aptos, Soquel and Zayante Indians inhabited the southern slopes of the Coastal Range, with unsurpassed views of the Pacific, and one particular small tribe, the Umunhum, perched atop a 3,442 foot mountain peak overlooking them all.

Being of a somewhat mild-mannered and unhurried nature, many of the valley Indians preferred to limit their agricultural endeavors to growing small patches of corn along the numerous creek banks. The corn was of a soft variety which could be easily ground into flour. This storable source of nourishment, along with seeds, oily pinenuts, roots, bulbs, berries, fish and wild game, and the all-important acorn combined to make the Indians' high protein diet.

California has about fifteen species of oaks, all of them generous acorn bearers. "Each fall," according to the Old Explorer in the National Geographic School Bulletin, "the average oak carpets the ground with upwards of 5,000 of the small nuts." In the old days, acorn gatherers were not limited to just the Indians - quail, pheasants, woodpeckers, squirrels, bears, deer, fox, raccoon, muskrats and mice also feasted on the "fruit of the oak."

Considered the staff of life for the California Indian, the acorn was a rich source of starch. According to reports of occasional foreign travelers on expeditions to the new world, however, after tasting the local diet, they found they "suffered great injury to their health, and also had indigestion and fever."

Harvest time was a family affair. Everyone helped, as more than 500 pounds of acorns were needed to feed the average Indian family for one year. The nuts were stored in special huts built up on platforms or in woven baskets on the shelves of the pit houses. As needed, they were shelled, either roasted or baked, and then pounded on flat stones.

By shaking the mealy residue through woven baskets, the fine meal was separated from the coarse. Then it was leached to remove the bitterness caused by tannic acid. This was accomplished by placing the meal in sieve-like baskets, and then letting bubbling stream water run through it for a period of time.

Indian women worked laboriously, up to this point, shelling, roasting, grinding, and leaching the meal, only to wind up with an end product that was rather tasteless and bland. To make it more palatable, the meal was then seasoned or mixed with red clay and made into a form of dough. If the dough was sun-dried, or baked in stone-lined earthen ovens, it became "pinole" or bread. Largely due to the clay additive, the bread, though tasty, had a tendency to turn as hard as a rock if not eaten within a day or so. If the dough, on the other hand, was thinned down somewhat and cooked, it became "attole" or mush. A sweetener, extracted from various shrubs and bulbs, was added to the attole to enhance the flavor.

There was fine fishing in these parts. Speckled trout and fresh-water salmon abounded in the rushing creeks to the point where catching them by hand was easy sport, although nets and baskets were also used. Mollusks from both the ocean and the bay were another favorite and plentiful source of food.

The valley Indians made good use of the wild animal tracks through the mountains on their numerous claming and fishing expeditions to the sea. They traversed the rugged precipitous grades as fast as any fleet-footed animal, further pounding out, over the years, a faintly recognizable trail 20 miles long, through the Santa Cruz Mountains. There is ample evidence today as to where the Indians most enjoyed hosting their fish and clambakes. All along the ridges of the summit there are still to be found tell-tale mounds of shells.

The Costanoan Indians were also skillful weapon makers, producing some implements of extraordinary craftsmanship and elegance. On their hunting expeditions into the foothills and mountains, they could bring down an elk, deer, antelope or bear with bow and arrow, or by the use of cunning disguises or traps. One very successful method of hunting deer was with the use of a decoy. The hunter wore the prepared head of a deer, the hide of which also partially covered his shoulders. The rest of his body was painted a tawny brown, and the disguise allowed him to creep well within range of his prey.

The Indians were pioneers in the art of barbecuing. Back in their villages or camps, after such an expedition, they would prepare their catch on spits set to sizzle over an open fire.

Deeply religious and filled with superstitions, the sun-worshipping Costanoan Indians also attached great significance to the giant redwoods of the Coastal Range. They believed their "Mana" or spirit of the gods, dwelt within these ancient, towering yet graceful trees. Small wonder, as they were awesome in appearance and rose to breathless heights of two to three hundred feet. But the mountains housed more than one spirit for the Indians. Stones, twigs, rushing brooks and fallen leaves, and, according to Brusa, the coyote, eagle and hummingbird - all were held sacred.

Not far from the natural gap, in another canyon of the Coastal Range located in what are now called the Gabilan Mountains, the local Indians discovered an amazing deposit of cinnabar. Cinnabar, the vermilion-colored ore from which quicksilver is extracted, was in great demand as it was used by the Indians in their ceremonial and war paints. As word about the discovery spread up and down the Pacific Coast, Indians came from great distances to obtain their supplies from the suddenly wealthy tribe that now monopolized the trade.

Not all those who came, came in peace. In many instances, the local Indians rightfully resented the "invasion" of other tribes into their mining operation. The resulting fierce battles fought over the precious cinnabar became known to history as the infamous and bloody "Vermilion Wars."

Recently, archeological findings indicate that in this particular area of the cinnabar find, the Indians were definitely more war-like than in other surrounding areas. The theory, based on studies of skeletal materials, claims that from ten to thirty percent of the Indians here met a violent death.

There were many Indian superstitions about New Almaden (the site of the discovery) and one of the most prevalent was that "Evil Spirits" killed all those who trespassed. The evil spirit, of course, came in the form of invisible, toxic fumes from the mercury which was present in such rich abundance that it actually collected in small liquid pools in the earth.

But the "Evil Spirit" not only attacked trespassers, it worked insidiously on those brave handsome warriors who persisted, over the years, in smearing their bodies so liberally with the prized, glistening red paste. Many died, frothing at the mouth and writhing in agony, before the Indians realized that the greatly feared "Evil Spirit" was contained in their precious, sought-after cinnabar.

According to William A. Wulf, prominent Los Gatos historian, not only were Indians from other areas lured here by the presence of cinnabar, but by the climate and scenic wonders, as well. For years, representatives of many Pacific Northwest tribes came from hundreds of miles away to visit their favorite "resort", the area now called Vasona.

Situated in the gently rolling foothills, just below the pass through the mountains leading over to the ocean beaches, this lush green meadow was richly endowed with oak trees, sweet clover and gushing streams. It is today a popular park, with a man-made lake and recreation area, but years ago, here, in tranquillity, the Indians would gather to visit, relax, hunt and fish.

Although it had endured for centuries, the Indians' relatively simple, peaceful way of life was about to come to an end. Since the days of Columbus, explorers from Europe had been making progress in claiming various parts of the New World for their governments. Spain was instrumental in colonizing the territory that was later to become California.

CHAPTER 3

ESTABLISHMENT OF THE SPANISH MISSIONS

Several El Camino Reals (also known as The King's Highway) emanated from Mexico City in different directions. One went southeast, into Central America, one southwest to Acapulco, and one went east to Vera Cruz. Two roads radiated in a northerly direction - the longest passed through San Antonio, Texas and then turned toward New Orleans, Louisiana, and terminated in St. Augustine, Florida. A branch off this road led to Santa Fe, New Mexico. But the one that concerns the development of the North American West was the El Camino Real that went over to the west coast of Mexico and proceeded north up into Arizona Territory, then turned west again toward San Diego, California.

In addition to Spain's military acquisitions spreading up from Mexico, the Franciscans (a religious order under Spanish commission headed by Father Junipero Serra) also began taking over the missions founded by the Jesuits a few years earlier. Father Serra's purpose was to put an end to the disputes which had arisen between the Spanish army, resident in California, and the Jesuit clergy governing the missions.

The missions, starting with the first built in San Diego, were planned about 20 or so miles apart along the King's Highway. They were built along the California Coast to just north of San Francisco. It was a good day's walk from one mission to the next, about the limit for the peripatetic Franciscan Fathers.

In an overt act of cooperation, Father de la Pena, a Franciscan priest, and Lieutenant Jose Joaquin Moraga, of the Spanish army, founded a mission together. It was the eighth in the series of original twenty-one. The mission was located near the west bank of the Guadalupe Creek, as it empties into the southern tip of San Francisco Bay. It was named after the founder of the Poor Sainte Clare's Order of Assisi, Italy, and was dedicated in the year 1777 - six months after the signing of the Declaration of Independence. The impact of the simple ceremony on the lives of the Indians was yet to be realized.

Unaccustomed as they were to any such large-scale "invasion", the Indians offered little or no resistance to their much more ambitious conquerors from the south. They allowed their lands to be confiscated and their huts destroyed. Within the confines of the mission, where many of them were moved, their high protein diet was replaced with one of a different nature. There was suddenly an abundance of meat - beef, oxen and mutton, in particular - but of a higher fat content than they were used to. And there were wheaten cakes, and puddings and porridges, and fresh vegetables in season.

Up until this point in time, the beautiful Santa Clara Valley had remained mostly untouched and untilled. The Franciscan Fathers, however, found the native Indians willing to learn and quite trainable, and so now gardens sprouted and flourished where once there were only the carpets of sweet clover.

At the suggestion of Don Felipe de Neve (the third Spanish Governor of the territory of California) to the controlling government in Mexico, nine soldiers, from the Presidio in San Francisco, who were skilled in agriculture, three laborers and two settlers were sent to further establish the community. Land surrounding the mission was partitioned off and distributed among them. Soon this first white settlement in the area became a busy and thriving institution.

Father Fermin Francisco de Lausen, historian William A. Wulf revealed in a Los Gatos newspaper article on November 15, 1977, was the President of the Franciscan Missions of California in the late 1700's. He performed the dedication ceremony of the Mission at Santa Cruz in the year 1791. He also made one of the first written references to the Franciscan trail in a letter to Don San Jose Antonio de Romeau of the San Carlos Mission, after he had walked the trail from Santa Cruz to Santa Clara - about 28 miles. "I returned to Santa Clara Mission by a road that was rougher, but it was also shorter and more direct. I made arrangements for repairing it by means of the Indians of the mission I just mentioned, and an excellent job has been done, because for that job, as for all others, the commandant of the Presidio of San Francisco, Don Hermenegildo Sal, furnished all the help that was asked, with all speed and promptness."

In 1797, permission was granted to move the mission settlement at Santa Clara to another site on higher ground. The relocation was to protect the community from the occasionally flooding Bay waters, and also the renegade Indians who, in refusing missionization, had turned to thievery, horse stealing, and other acts of annoyance. The mission buildings, as they were originally situated, were an easy target for such disasters and mischief.

Sporadic Indian raids continued in spite of the move, but now they were not always successful. The punishment for such acts of crime was swift and severe, and many times, permanent. According to a news article, the Indian, Yoscolo, made the mistake of raiding the relocated Santa Clara Mission storehouse, before he fled the compound, coaxing several hundred other Indians at the same time to follow him into the foothills of the Santa Cruz Mountains for refuge. The renegades were finally tracked down, defeated, and Yoscolo captured. He was executed immediately, and his head staked in front of the mission as a reminder to other Indians that "crime does not pay."

In contrast to Yoscolo, Marcelo Pico, a giant of an Indian of Aztec descent, standing six feet tall or more and weighing close to 250 pounds, became a leader and a sexton in the Santa Clara Mission. He and his 1,500 followers did most of the work on the mission buildings. They set out grape vines brought up from Baja California by Father Serra, and fruit trees (apple, apricot, peach, pear, cherry) and planted over 200 magnificent shade trees along The Alameda, the still popular "avenue" now connecting the two cities of San Jose and Santa Clara. As a reward for their hard work, Marcelo and his tribesmen were allowed to choose homesites from a generous land area. This area extended from the Mission out to Almaden, and from the Guadalupe Creek up to the summit of the Santa Cruz Mountains.

Two years after Mexico had been formed into a republic, Mexican governmental authorities began to interfere with the rights of the Franciscan Fathers and the affairs of state in California. First, the missions were denied their substantial monetary aid, and the Fathers were suddenly put upon to raise their own funds. Then, in 1826, instructions were sent to the authorities in California for the liberation of the Indians. And finally, claiming that the missions were never intended to be permanent, the Mexican federal officials ordered the missions be secularized (i.e., removed from under Church control). With all these confusing events, which they did not understand, the Mission Indians became fretful and thin. More and more often they gazed sadly toward their "Blue Mountains" - always there, waiting in the distance. The Indians longed desperately for the life they once knew.

Within a few years, the dedicated work of the Fathers was completely destroyed. In 1834, 1,800 Indians had been cared for in the Santa Clara Mission, but by 1842, only 400 remained. Many drifted away, refusing to maintain the fertile, productive lands that had been returned to them. Others died of pneumonia, smallpox, and other unheard of diseases.

For those who remained, the death of their beloved Father Catala, then head of the Santa Clara Mission, was the last straw. The Indians had traditionally cremated their dead, along with their finery and most prized possessions, so that the soul could readily escape to heaven. The thought of their dear and kindly friend being buried in the ground, "toward Purgatory" they felt, sent them into a frenzy.

The following story, not founded on fact, has been told and written in various ways over recent years. If not true, one thing it does is point out the tragic plight of a once proud and self-sufficient people whose destiny had been changed forever:

In the following early morning hours, before dawn, the enraged Marcelo and several faithful members of his Aztec tribe, silently slipped out of the Mission compound. They carried only a few meager possessions on their backs. Crossing Stevens Creek, they proceeded up along Quito Trail to a ridge above the future site of the town to be named Los Gatos. From there, the Indians cut up through the gap into the foothills. Closer and closer they came to their old neglected homesites, up the unbelievably steep, rugged canyon to the summit. Their destination was just beyond, a hollowed-out redwood stump of mammoth proportions which was formed, in actuality, by a semi-circular stand of a dozen trees, their roots and trunks impossibly entwined. This secluded wonder, over 150 feet around, had served years before as their Sun God's Sanctuary.

Once there, Marcelo, it is written, threw his crucifix onto the ground in disillusionment, trading it for a supple willow branch. This he twisted into a circle and held it high. Then the Indians clasped hands and gazed toward the zenith, praying for understanding, forgiveness, and perhaps the strength to endure the desolate and declining years ahead. (Marcelo did eventually return to the fold. It is reported that he lived well past 100 years of age within the protection of the crumbling mission walls.)

Descendants of these people who still live in and about the San Francisco Bay Area have never liked the term "Costanoan", thrust on them by the Spaniards. They prefer to be called by their self-given name of Ohlone.

* * *

Starting in San Diego and progressing up the California Coast to just north of San Francisco are 21 missions as listed in the "National Geographic School Bulletin", November 17, 1969. They were built, but not in exact geographic order, along the El Camino Real a hard day's journey apart. Today they "leave a lasting Spanish imprint" around which major cities have grown.

Name of Mission	*Year Founded*
San Diego de Alcala	*1769*
San Luis Rey de Francia	*1798*
San Juan Capistrano	*1776*
San Gabriel Arcangel	*1771*
San Fernando Rey de Espana	*1797*
San Buenaventura	*1782*
Santa Barbara	*1786*
Santa Ines	*1804*
La Purisima Concepcion	*1787*
San Luis Obispo de Tolosa	*1772*
San Miguel Arcangel	*1797*
San Antonio de Padua	*1771*
Nuestra Senora de la Sol	*1791*
San Carlos Borromeo del Carmelo	*1770*
San Juan Bautista	*1797*
Santa Cruz	*1791*
Santa Clara de Asis	*1777*
San Jose de Guadalupe	*1797*
San Francisco de Asis	*1776*
San Rafael Arcangel	*1817*
San Francisco Solano	*1823*

El Camino Real

CHAPTER 4

CATTLE RANCHING - A WAY OF LIFE

But even as one way of life was dying, a youthful new vigorous one was beginning to develop in the Santa Clara Valley. Many of the native Californians were now half-caste between Castilian and Indian. Primarily, the men were vaqueros (cowboys) and cattle ranchers, spending a great deal of time in the saddle. They were a good-natured, generous and hospitable people but many times moved to a strange fierceness and cruelty especially when excited. They loved to dance and sing. Sometimes, when they were not working the herds, and with two or three men astride each horse, they would ride through town, strumming guitars and serenading the local citizenry. When the mood was right, the high-spirited men would spur their prancing horses right through the swinging doors and into the business establishments! And knowing full well the dark side of their personalities, what proprietor would deny them entrance?

The expansive areas outside of the town of San Jose had turned into valuable grazing land. For a small sum of money, if one was of reputable character, a grant of land was possible. "Espediente" or Petition Papers for the desired area, along with the "Diseno", which was a rough survey map, had to be presented to the Mexican Government in Monterey, according to William Wulf. When granted, these domains were called Ranchos and were measured in Mexican Leagues. Even though they were surveyed, they were rarely enclosed by fences, and simply extended from one land mark to another.

Each spring, various ranchos would host "rodeos" which were much more work than show in those days. Hand-dug ditches, defining some of the property lines, were not very effective in keeping the cattle from roaming about freely, sometimes 50 to 60 miles away. So the purpose of the annual rodeo, amid much whooping, hollering and raising of dust, was to cut one's own brand from the herd and head them for home. After each rancher had accomplished this task, also taking along any new-born calves that followed their mothers, the host was then awarded all the calves and other unmarked cattle left behind.

In the market place, two-year-old heifers, used for breeding, brought $ 3.00, and a plump steer, delivered, sold for $ 3.50. At these prices, the nasty business of cattle rustling also blossomed.

The "matanza" or killing of the cattle began shortly after the dust from the rodeos had settled. The number butchered annually was dependent on the number of new-born calves, and how many cattle could be properly fed and cared for. After the butchering, the hides were cut and treated for export, bringing $ 1.50 in cash, or equivalent $ 2.00 in goods. Soap was made from the animal fat, and the prime cuts of meat were shredded and laid out in the sun to dry into a form of jerky.

From the Watkins Song Book, circa 1930, compliments of the J. R. Watkings Company.

CHAPTER 5

EARLY COOKING

As cooks, many of the women in the area were unsurpassed. Their slow simmering pots of beef and beans, liberally laced with hot peppers, were aromatic and full of flavor. They were also experts in the art of making tortillas - a kind of unleavened bread which could be made from either wheat or corn. The maize (or grain) they used was first boiled in a weak lye solution over wood ashes, and then ground into a paste between two smooth stones. For each tortilla, a small portion of dough was repeatedly slapped against a bare thigh or adeptly thrown from one hand to the other, back and forth, back and forth, until the round, flat, wafer-thin shape of the tortilla was finally attained. The tortillas were then placed on a flat iron and baked over a fire.

When the women weren't busy making tortillas, they were helping to thresh the grain for them. This process involved throwing the grain upon the floor of the corral and letting the mares and their colts trample out the seed. As questionable a practice as this might sound, it was claimed to be more sanitary than many of the newfangled processing systems being developed "back East."

Then, by tossing the grain and chaff into the air with long wooden forks, the chaff was eventually blown away, with the desired grain left behind on the ground. On a good windy day, several bushels could be winnowed in this fashion.

According to a publication entitled "The Original Mexicans": "The tortilla can be served at any meal and between meals as a snack as well. At breakfast it is usually served soft and warm. For lunch it can be fried and used with a topping to become a tostada. For snacks it can be fried folded and filled as a taco. The evening meal can be a sauce-dipped, rolled, and stuffed tortilla called an enchilada..... Certainly there are many more variations for the use of the tortilla."

In Mexico proper, two families greatly influenced the flavor and methods of preparing foods. Once again according to the above reference, "In 1795, Jose Maria Guadalupe de Cuervo, a man with a keen mind and a particularly astute sense of business, obtained from the administration of Guadalajara the right to make mezcal (wine) - or, as we know it today Tequila...."

"Toward the later part of the 18th century there is a record of a Jose Ortega. Jose was a Castilian - his home the high land of central and northern Spain. When in the early 1770's, an expedition was being organized by Jean Bautista de Anza, Jose quickly agreed to join that adventure. The result, in 1776, was the founding of a Spanish Presidio on San Francisco Bay. At this point some years passed before the records of the Ortega family resumed. They did so in the person of Emile Ortega, a direct descent of Jose, who began to interest himself in the commercial preparation and canning of green chiles. These chiles and their sauces have played so important a part in Mexican and Californian style food."

The Legend of Turkey Mole'

The legend surrounding mole', and how it came to be, is inspirational. The story disproves many an old adage, like "you can't make a silk purse out of a sow's ear."

A few hundred years ago, a traveling Bishop was about to arrive at a poor convent somewhere in Baja California. The nuns were in a flurry of excitement as there was not much time to prepare nor did they have anything in their pantry with which to fix a meal befitting the occasion. Mother Superior encouraged them with a prayer, and the nuns set to work. Everything but the kitchen sink went into the mole' (in order to make enough to go around). The varied ingredients, which included everything from left-over pieces of wild turkey breast, onions, a handful of vegetables, chili peppers, and even a piece of chocolate, were tossed into the pot.

The Bishop was so impressed with the final outcome (and fortunately hungry), that he demanded the recipe, and its popularity began to spread as he continued his journeys. And the Sisters? Well, they passed into culinary history.

CHAPTER 6

SPORTING EVENTS

Although the native Californians did not drink much alcohol, if any, they did have one vice - gambling. The favorite game was "monte" based on the principles of banking, and it became an obsession with many of them. According to one delightful account in THE HISTORY OF SANTA CLARA COUNTY, "Even on Sundays while the women were in church and the priest was attending the altar, the men would be outside, with their cards and money spread out on blankets. To them, gambling was no sin, even though many times they had to take out loans at an outrageous 12-1/2 % per day, mortgage their land, sell their livestock, and sometimes, even their wives' clothing."

The account goes on that bullfights, especially on Sunday in front of the church, were not uncommon in these parts, either. And when a grizzly bear (still roaming in the Santa Cruz Mountains nearby) could be obtained, the action became even more blood-thirsty. The animals were tethered and staked - but close enough to one another for the action to take place. The snarling, snorting beasts would then battle it out until one or the other was killed or both refused to continue the assault. Generally, and perhaps surprisingly, it was the bull who emerged victorious. This bloody custom was finally brought to an end when the California legislature imposed an act in 1854 to prevent "noisy and barbarous amusements on the Sabbath." Heavy fines were levied on those entrepreneurs who continued the practice, finally putting a definite damper on the sport.

The Pueblo de San Jose had become the first civil settlement in Alta, or Upper, California back in 1777, with the establishment of the Mission and minuscule community around it. A rather crude system of government existed in the village. A mayor, of sorts, maintained the 'judicial' system without any precedents, books or lawyers to fall back on for advice.

Fifty-four years later, in the year 1831, a simple census, was taken. It indicated that there were "166 men, 145 women, 104 boys, and 110 girls - a grand total of 525 of Spanish, Mexican and Indian descent."

In all of California, about this same time, it was estimated there were only 100 "foreigners." Most of these adventurers and soldiers of fortune came by ship, and "fate and chance decided where they would settle." For the most part, they befriended the native Californians, accepted their customs and way of life, and even married into their families.

By this time, though, more and more overland trails were being explored and opened by a growing number of hardy pioneers. Oregon had lured many of them, but some, when they reached the imposing Sierra Nevada Mountains, and heard intriguing tales of the still "foreign country" known as California, turned their horses and wagons in that direction.

CHAPTER 7

JOHN FREMONT ARRIVES IN CALIFORNIA

Governor Juan Alvarado was appointed to rule California from 1836 to 1842. During this time, a revolution took place within Mexico itself, causing major shifts and changes within the government, and problems as far north as San Jose, California. It reached the point where the civil command of Alvarado, and the military authorities, under the leadership of General Mariano Vallejo, could rarely agree on anything. But when the two men realized that an appointee from Mexico, a certain General Micheltorena, had been sent secretly for the purpose of taking away their powers, they set aside their bickering and formed an alliance. In a bold move, they declared California "independent" from Mexico. Along with the assistance of General Jose Castro, they forced the intrepid spy, Micheltorena, to retreat and eventually to leave the territory.

In 1844, the plot began to thicken once more with the arrival of Captain John C. Fremont of the United States Army. He was sent West by the U.S. Government for the purpose of exploration, topographical studies, and land acquisition. Now that overland travel was becoming more feasible and popular, the U.S. Government was interested, indeed, in exploring this Mexican territory known as the "far out West!"

Fremont led a company of sixty-two men, including Kit Carson and six Delaware Indians. Earlier, Fremont had attempted an expedition to the West in search of a plausible route to the Pacific Coast, but this adventure had only taken him as far west as the Rocky Mountains. According to William Maule, in a re-print of an original historical article published in the Gardnerville (Nevada) Record Courier, "In 1843, Fremont regrouped and made what is now referred to as the Second Expedition." This attempt took the party past the Rockies and over to the backside of the Sierra Nevada Mountains. The men studied the mountains facing them from a camp on the East Walker River, west of Mason Valley, Nevada, and north of what is now Bridgeport, California. They were up against some of the most formidable peaks in the Sierra Range with sheer walls of granite 10,000 feet and higher above sea level and topped with many jagged sawtooth prominence!

Fortunately, for the Fremont party, severe winter weather conditions forced their expedition from this vantage point to a more sheltered site further north. This was near the future site of the small town of Markleeville, close to the California-Nevada border. Some local Indians, of a friendly nature, joined the men around their campfire. They informed the weary and hungry explorers that a few months earlier a group of white men had found their way over the Sierra from this point. The Indians were referring to Bidwell-Bartleson, the first Overland Immigrant Party.

After unbelievable hardships, where once they were reduced to eating a stew made of dying mule and dog with the last of the dried peas thrown in, the nearly-starved Fremont party reached the summit and found where the mountain streams flowed - at long last - toward the Pacific!

Today, this pass is named for Kit Carson, Fremont's trusted guide. At the summit, a marker stands with a replica of his name carved into a tree trunk at the time of their passage in 1844.

* * *

Coming into the San Jose area on horseback, one of Fremont's first visits was to the New Almaden Quicksilver Mines. He surveyed the operation, estimated its value at about $ 20,000 dollars, and sent immediate word back to Washington. Then he asked the Mexican military commander, General Castro, for provisions for his party of men. He also requested permission to pass through the area unmolested. He received a verbal grant to do so but shrugged off the need to put it in writing. Instead of "passing through", however, Fremont decided to cut over the Santa Cruz Mountains and go on down to Monterey, the seat of the Mexican government in Alta California.

Back in San Jose, General Castro became quite uneasy when he got wind of this unexpected and highly suspicious move. He sent one of his scouts along the "road to Santa Cruz" near which Fremont and his men were encamped for the night on property owned by Edward Petty Hartwell. Under Castro's orders, the scout accused Fremont on a trumped-up charge of horse stealing, and presented him with a summons.

With a cool head and steady hand, Fremont replied to the false accusation in writing, denying the charges. He claimed it would be impossible to make a personal appearance in San Jose since he was under orders from the United States Government to proceed. Then he boldly marched his men toward the mountains straight ahead and, supposedly, crossed the gap at the point where Los Gatos Creek enters the valley.

On March 1st, Captain Fremont and his men encamped on the rancho known as Laguna Seca, owned by Captain William Fisher, and it was here that Fremont was the recipient of yet another charge that he had "entered towns and villages in contempt of the laws of the Mexican Government." He was ordered to leave the country in lieu of "compulsory measures."

After the messenger had left, Fremont, once again ignoring the orders and threats, led his small company to the top of Hawk's Peak, a 2,000 foot mountain in the rough terrain of the Gabilans. Here, about thirty miles from Monterey, the men felled trees and hurriedly constructed a crude fort. The Stars and Stripes, nailed to a flagpole, snapped smartly in the breeze forty feet above the ground.

These bold moves had not gone unnoticed, however. Fremont had been under constant surveillance by a Mexican scout sent out of Monterey. The spy scrambled back to his superiors, reporting his observations.

Under the leadership of Don Jose, 200 men and two small caliber cannons were dispatched out of Monterey into the mountains. The encounter was later described in the memoirs of one of Fremont's lieutenants. As it appears in THE HISTORY OF THE SANTA CLARA VALLEY:

"Don Jose was rather in the humor of the King of France, who with 20,000 men, marched up the hill and then marched down again."

Fremont and his men, armed for battle, waited impatiently for an attack that, inexplicably, never came. Finally tiring of the cat and mouse game, Fremont marched his men silently out of their fort late one night, and east into the San Joaquin Valley, some distance away. When Don Jose's scout discovered the fort deserted the following morning, the surprise (and no doubt disappointment) was overwhelming.

Word was sent immediately to Castro in San Jose who, on the other hand, was quite elated. Without going into detail, he wrote to Mexico that his promise to drive Fremont from the country had been fulfilled "in glorious victory."

Governor Pio Pico, down in Los Angeles, began to distrust and despise the more and more frequent arrivals of the white man, regardless of his purpose. And the new American settlers throughout the territory felt the animosity with apprehension.

Mexico, however, was not supporting the territory of California mainly because of problems and confusion within its own internal affairs. It was costly to send arms and support such a great distance, and so, in spite of Pico's fears and dire predictions, there was no aid forthcoming. The great territory now looked to be up for grabs among the four very interested and vying forces - the United States, France, Great Britain and Russia!

The Russians, as a matter of fact, had even established a fortress and stronghold 80 miles north of San Francisco on the Pacific Coast. In a San Jose News article by Jack Schreibman, dated May 10, 1977, "For 29 years beginning in 1812, the Russians and their helpers built and maintained Fort Ross." The stated intent of their colonization was to "gather pelts of the sea otter and produce food to support their fishing expeditions in Alaska." At one time "there were 700 persons and 50 out buildings at and surrounding Fort Ross." Academicians of Russian history, however, feel that the true intent of the Russians 'being' there was to study and explore Northern California, and establish a stronghold. They did accomplish much surveying, naming rivers, tributaries and mountains (like Mount Shasta, derived from the Russian word "Shastia" which means "good luck"). They built a shipyard, learned about the Indians, and "conducted a lively commerce with the Spaniards and others."

According to Schreibman, many theories exist on the reasons the Russians abandoned Fort Ross, suddenly, in 1841, as white settlers were moving into the territory. Some believe they did not want to get involved with the Mexican revolutionaries who were pressuring them. Others say it was simply economics, and still others believe it was Great Britain who forced them to abandon their California outpost. At any rate, the "Russians left Fort Ross after selling out to the Swiss adventurer John Sutter for $30,000."

A disappointed Governor Pio Pico advised sadly that if California had to indeed be given up, that it be annexed to either France or England, and most certainly, *NOT* the United States. General Castro agreed.

General Vallejo, on the other hand, was steadfastly opposed to Pico and Castro's views. He could hardly bear the thought of California being handed over to a foreign monarchy. If Mexico, herself, could no longer support the territory, he had his doubts that any European interest could manage better from even a greater distance. Vallejo advised annexation to the United States, and predicted marvelous changes would be in store. "California," he claimed, "will grow strong and flourish, and her people will be prosperous, happy and free."

Vallejo was not the only one in California with such sentiments. A small band of Americans, about this time, was bravely determined to declare California's independence, and raised a flag of its own (the famous "Bear Flag") on June 14, 1846, in the town of Sonoma. About the same time, Captain John Fremont was ordered by the U.S. Government, to clear Northern California of all hostile Mexicans.

General Castro called it a contemptible act and a daring invasion. "There is still time," he proclaimed angrily, "for us to rise en masse!"

But even greater plans than this were already in the making. The United States had declared War on Mexico, which lasted two years. The City of Mexico had already been captured, and Commodore John Drake Sloat of the United States Navy, was approaching California's Monterey Peninsula by sea. On July 7, 1846, without much resistance, Monterey fell to the Americans, and the Stars and Stripes were raised over the town.

General Castro, with a great deal of reluctance, read Sloat's victory statement out of Monterey to his troops stationed near San Jose:

> *"I declare to the inhabitants of California, that although I come in arms with a powerful force, I do not come as an enemy to California.*
> *"With full confidence in the honor and integrity of the inhabitants of the country, I invite the judges, alcaldes (mayors), and other civil officers to execute their functions as heretofore, that the public tranquillity be not disturbed, at least until the government of the territory can be definitely arranged.*
> *"All persons holding titles to real estate, or in quiet possession of lands under color or right, shall have these titles guaranteed to them..."*

General Vallejo reinforced the new government's stand. "Look not with jealousy," he said prophetically, "upon the hardy pioneers who scale our mountains and cultivate our unoccupied plains, but rather welcome them as brothers, who come to share with us a common destiny."

CHAPTER 8

ARRIVAL OF THE WHITE SETTLERS

And come they did - the fur trappers, sailors and "soldiers of fortune" of many nationalities to settle the area in and around San Jose. Today we recognize the names of many of them because of the towns, schools, and streets dedicated in their honor - John Gilroy, Robert Livermore, Isaac Branham, Josiah Belden - to name only a few. Belden, incidentally, was with the Bidwell-Bartleson Company, the aforementioned first Overland Immigrant Party, and became one of the early merchants in San Jose. In 1843, three white women arrived with their pioneering husbands, and in 1846, nearly all the surviving members of the ill-fated Donner Party also settled in the area.

Another of the first white settlers on record in the area was a young sea captain by the name of Willard M. Hanks. Hanks had endured unbelievable hardships as a youth, after he had run away from his New London, Connecticut home. His adventure-filled saga eventually brought him to California in the 1830's, and he was so impressed with the area that he temporarily gave up his life on the high seas. In order to stay in California, however, in the year 1838, Hanks discovered it was necessary to become a Mexican citizen. And the easiest way for a "foreigner" to satisfy that technicality was to marry a Californian of Spanish descent. Hanks chose a pretty young Mexican girl by the name of Isabella for his bride. Then, there was a second requirement. In order for the marriage, itself, to take place, Hanks had to become a member of the Catholic Church. This he did willingly, accepting his new Baptismal name of "Julian."

Captain Willard M. "Julian" Hanks became a prominent businessman and much respected citizen of San Jose. But he and Isabella were eventually drawn from the downtown section to the quiet, remote foothills of the Santa Cruz Mountains. They built a cabin home in the vicinity of the gap (later called Lexington), and here they raised their family. Hanks involved himself primarily with the development of his land but continued active in California politics.

They had seen many drastic changes in just the few short years since their marriage. Suddenly, with the United States victorious at the end of the two-year war with Mexico, it was the native Mexican residents in California who were considered a conquered people. By an act of Congress, these true and naturalized citizens had actually been declared the "foreigners!"

Willard and Isabella were able to survive the legalities and even took a positive part in these suddenly upsetting and major changes, as did many others who found themselves in similar situations. But by 1848, with the great Mexican land grants beginning to break up, there were thousands of other Mexicans, now unemployed, who discovered themselves to be displaced persons. They barely understood what had happened to them. Many, in anger and frustration, turned to outlawry. Others simply drifted away.

Another of the early settlers was James Alexander Forbes. He was born in Inverness, Scotland, of a wealthy, cultured family but decided, as a young college graduate, to migrate to America. He shipped out, as a 4th-class mate, aboard the whaling ship "Fanny", arriving in Yerba Buena - San Francisco in 1831.

Historian William Wulf, who has done extensive research on the Forbes' family, recounts the following story which is a gripping tale of "reversal of fortune", beginning with the eager and enterprising James locating himself in the beautiful Santa Clara Valley. He met and married Maria Ana Galindo (as her name appears on the wedding registry at the Mission Santa Clara). She was the daughter of a prominent Spanish family. Her father, Juan Christomo Galindo, was the Major-domo of the Mission. Together Maria and James began to raise a large family - 12 children in all. And James began to pursue his many interests such as music and languages, and other ventures such as politics and real estate.

Wulf continues, in 1846, James and the last Franciscan Priest at Mission Santa Clara, Padre Real, joined with the first owners, the Robles Brothers, since 1824, to develop and operate which was then called the New Almaden Quicksilver Mines. In 1849, Forbes' uncle, Alexander Forbes of Tepic, Mexico, came for a visit and to inspect the mines which young James had written him about. He was impressed and purchased and took control over the mines himself.

In 1851, James persuaded the Jesuit Missionaries to come down to Mission Santa Clara for the express purpose of starting a college and school. Here he intended to enroll his nine sons. Upon arrival, the Missionaries found that Forbes was living in some of the Mission buildings and would not move out until he was paid the sum of $ 11,000.00! Out of this he purchased bricks and lumber to start the construction of his mansion behind the mission and paid $ 3,000.00 back to the Missionaries towards the education fees of his sons!

In 1853, James took out a loan for $ 100,000.00 from "an old man in Guadalajara, Mexico", at an interest rate of 3 % per month! About the same time, James had also drawn up the architectural plans for an innovative flour mill which he built, probably using a good portion of his $ 100,000.00, on the east bank of Los Gatos Creek. Unfortunately, the four-story building, constructed entirely of local timbers and beautiful stones found in and about the creek bed, was beset with problems from the start. James did not have a clue as to how the massive machinery would fit inside the building. These plans were not drawn up until December 1, 1855, almost two years after the fact.

James, who was now in dire financial straits, had to then take out two additional loans, in the amount of $ 30,000.00, from Gustave Touchard, a San Francisco fine furniture and rug dealer who had furnished Forbes' mansion, in order to just pay the interest on the original note. But Forbes was unable then to pay even the interest on the most recent loans, and on May 29, 1857, the Santa Rosa Brand Flour Mill, and the 2,000 acre Santa Rosa Rancho, and all the portion of Rancho Rinconada de Los Gatos east of Los Gatos Creek, which James owned, had to be sold at a Santa Clara County Sheriff's Sale. It went for $ 28,613.00, to a certain Gustave Touchard, who subsequently sold it off over the next 30 years at a great profit!

To add to James' grief, his uncle Alexander had been chased out of Tepic, Mexico, after being caught shipping gold and silver from his mines out of San Blas, Mexico, to San Francisco without paying either an inland tax or an export tax. It had been James' job to deposit this wealth in the bank but, unfortunately, he was spending it as fast as it came in. By 1856 all avenues of financial aid had been cut off, and James was forced into bankruptcy.

Strangely enough, after it was completed correctly the Santa Rosa Brand Flour Mill began to flourish. But it passed into other hands and then stood idle and abandoned for years - close to one hundred, as a matter of fact.

In the year 1950, Wulf concludes, Forbes' Mill was made a California State Landmark, and the Los Gatos Preservation Society had it placed on the United States Register of Historic Buildings. It still stands today, as a museum, and is acknowledged as the oldest building in Los Gatos.

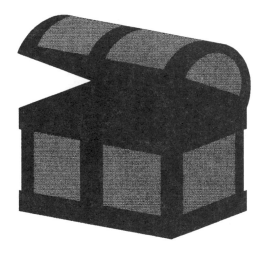

Forbes Mill

Built in 1853 by James Alexander Forbes, this is the oldest building in Los Gatos. Originally a 4-story structure built with local stone and lumber, it served as the Santa Rosa Brand Flour Mill before falling into other ownership. It stood idle and abandoned for years but today it is a museum and a Registered Historical Landmark.

CHAPTER 9

THE GOLD RUSH YEARS

According to the California Guide, there were more than 1000 murders during the Gold Rush years of 1849 - 1856, with only one known conviction.

The California-Nevada Gold Rush, in 1848, has been described by many historians as "Bigger than Life." Men, not only throughout California, but across the country and around the world, left their homes and wives and children for no more than mere dreams of wealth. San Francisco became a booming port city with shiploads of would-be miners arriving weekly. Many seamen left their vessels to rot in the harbor while they headed for the High Sierra. From San Jose, there was an excited mass exodus toward such newly named locations as Angel's Camp, Sutter's Creek and French Gulch. Once-responsible ranchers and farmers left behind their livestock and a valley of grain just freshly planted.

By the fall of 1848, nearly all of the male population of the Santa Clara Valley had left for what was referred to as the Mother Lode, an area so abundant with gold that it could be panned for in the creeks and dug from the earth with a pick and shovel. Only the women, children, the elderly and those too ill to travel remained behind. Business began to stagnate, and when the grain harvest failed, the price of food skyrocketed. Butter jumped to over a $ 1.00 a pound, milk to $ 1.00 a quart, and eggs up to $ 3.00 a dozen! Reports of some failures to find gold in the Sierra were discounted in favor of the few success stories which filtered back. The left-behind residents dug in, hung on, and waited for more news from their loved ones.

According to Richard Erdoes, in his book SALOONS OF THE OLD WEST, there was a dearth of women in San Francisco in the spring of 1849. The way there by ship was just too arduous, and the overland immigrant trails were only beginning to open up. Husbands usually preceded their wives, trying to establish themselves before they sent for the rest of the family, which meant an over-abundance of males. By 1850, however, a few brave wives made the trip and were joined by "mail order wives" arriving sight unseen. As one miner put it, "she ain't nothin' for a drinkin' man to look at, but she sure can cook an' keep house. So I kept her." Erdoes continues, "There was a great demand for women, and so short the supply, that Mrs. Eliza Farnham decided to bring out from the East, as a commercial venture, two hundred cultured, educated, refined and respectable females. When she finally got to California, she was left with only three of these rarest of creatures."

Strangely enough, during these tumultuous times, the town of San Jose began to grow! Because it was already such an established community, and so conveniently located, other would-be miners and adventurers from far off places brought their families to San Jose before heading for the gold fields themselves. The new arrivals lived in tents, or thrown-together wood and adobe shacks, and made-do with primitive utensils and tools. Surprisingly, in spite of the hardships, they did establish themselves. They also fell in love with the area while waiting for their wandering men to come home.

When placer mining became less profitable as the surface gold to be found dwindled, another strike at Virginia City, Nevada, lured the miners further east and up into the high desert country. At its peak, during the gold rush years, the population of Virginia City mushroomed from practically zero to over 10,000 people, and the Comstock Mine produced over a million dollars a month in a combination of gold and silver. According to Wells Fargo history, the Wells Fargo Company Express and Banking handled the transportation and protection of the miners' gold from the Mother Lode to San Francisco. That was the express part of their business. In the city they exchanged the gold for money which was the banking side of the business. In those days, express and banking services went hand in hand.

The original owner, Henry "Pancake" Comstock, never got to see the full development of his mine, or the express and banking business that followed, since he sold out his ownership too soon, for a paltry $ 11,000 dollars. Later, after the mine began to produce its vast fortune in precious metals, Comstock took his life over his ill-timed real estate transaction, leaving only his name as a legacy.

The Comstock Mine was unique, however along with the later strikes at Bodie, California and adjacent Aurora, Nevada. While these mines boomed bringing in untold millions of dollars, many other such promising mines and ventures failed miserably. And as they did, disillusioned fortune hunters returned sheepishly home, admitting to no one that sometimes all they made was pocket change a day in their own personal search for gold. They were then faced with the monumental task of picking up the threads of their lives and starting over.

Claim Jumping was a most serious offense and probably accounted for the 1000 murders.

CHAPTER 10

THIEVES AND RUSTLERS

Back in the Santa Clara Valley, unemployment was high and dissatisfaction and confusion reigned, especially among the displaced Mexicans. Gangs of dissidents built up through the territory. Thieves and rustlers made an organized business of running off cattle, stealing horses, robbing saloons and stores, and holding up lone travelers, relieving them of their purses, other valuables, and on occasion, even their lives.

Without a doubt, one of the most infamous and yet romanticized figures in all of California history was Joaquin Murrietta. His craze for vengeance won him a fearful reputation throughout California in a very short period of time. In his early days, before the attack on his wife (which supposedly turned him outlaw) he worked as an accountant on one of San Jose's largest dairy farms, and was even a school teacher for a time. Then his pretty young wife was abused and ravaged by a group of drunken miners coming down out of the Sierra. From that moment on, Joaquin, in seeking his revenge, formed gangs (at least four), headed by brothers and cousins. Then began a bloody rampage that extended from border to border.

The trouble with outlaws was their wiliness. Many boasted, probably on purpose, similar names, attire and drooping mustaches, which may account for historical confusion regarding their whereabouts, exploits and ultimate demise. Stories of Joaquin's acts of violence spread rapidly by word of mouth, but were so embroidered upon and grossly exaggerated that his presence around the territory was spread rather thin. His gangs probably added to the illusion that he was in more than one place at the same time. Confusing reports had him driving 50 head of stolen cattle in the San Joaquin Valley, while simultaneously relieving a wayfarer of his purse 200 miles away!

Although he fashioned himself after Robin Hood, occasionally helping the rancheros with gifts of money and other kindness', his other acts became more atrocious, creating a legend of unequaled proportions.

It was an alarmed citizenry that cried, "Something must be done!" As one story goes, a WANTED poster offering a reward of $ 5,000 went up. A few days later, the following spine-tingling graffiti was found scrawled beneath the printed words:

"I will give $ 10,000!"
(signed) Joaquin Murrietta

And, finally there was Manuel Garcia, also known as "Three Fingered Jack", or in Spanish, "Tres Dedos." He ran with the Murrietta gang and robbed, killed and escaped at such an envious pace other banditos were hard-pressed to keep up. Unfortunately, there was much fiction confused with fact regarding this desperado, but apparently he met a violent death, also at an early age, about the same time as Joaquin himself.

A Gruesome Tale of Retribution

According to Lea F. McCarty in THE GUNFIGHTERS, "Captain Harry Love, a noted Los Angeles gunfighter, with 20 men, rode down upon the bandit (Joaquin Murrietta) surprising him at a campfire near Lake Tulare." Other accounts corroborate this, also indicating that the feared Tres Dedos was among the compromised gang members. They were summarily executed, and the head of Joaquin and the identifying hand of Manuel Garcia were severed and carried off to the Sheriff's Office from whence they were later auctioned.

Supposedly the new owner had them preserved in jars of alcohol and put on display in San Francisco. For twenty-five cents, morbid curiosity seekers could gaze upon them. The attraction drew thousands of people until the 1906 earthquake when the jars toppled from their shelves and their contents were lost forever.

CHAPTER 11

EARLY GOVERNMENT IN CALIFORNIA

Up until 1849, there still was no form of overall government in California other than that provided by the U.S. military forces. And the military commander entirely agreed with the populace that four years of military rule, especially since the war with Mexico had ended, was too much. On June 3, 1849, a special proclamation was issued calling for a convention. Delegates from each district were elected to attend. There were six from San Jose, one of whom was Captain Julian Hanks.

The convention met in Monterey on September 1, 1849, and lasted six weeks. Since there were very few precedents, and a scarcity of reference books, the Delegates worked very hard to hammer out, and frame, the first original Constitution of California. While the meeting was in session, residents of San Jose elected a two-man committee to go to Monterey and try to persuade the Delegates to name San Jose as the first State Capitol. They promised to have a suitable building ready and available by December - three months away. This was a risky promise, seeing as how there was no such building in existence in San Jose or anywhere nearby!

There was strong opposition to the San Jose proposal from the president of the convention who hailed from Benicia, about 50 miles northeast. The other Delegates approved, however, and San Jose was actually selected as the site for the first State Capitol. But a combination of events in the years 1849-1850, proved to be the beginning of the end of the San Jose dream. The most disruptive in the scheme of things was the weather. Torrential rains fell that winter, making travel nearly impossible. Even if Delegates could reach Alviso by boat at the southern tip of the San Francisco Bay, they could not disembark! The major road to the new State Assembly Hall was usually a sea of slick adobe mud into which horses, wagons and coaches sank. Many times travel came to a complete stand-still. According to noted area historian Leonard McKay, the Legislature, tiring of the mess, shortsightedly refusing to believe it would ever end, and tiring of the boredom brought on by the lack of anything "cultural" to do, began to consider other locations for the State Capitol. Perhaps in retaliation, the citizenry nicknamed this particular group of men "The Legislature of a Thousand Drinks", feeling they spent far too much time complaining and drinking in the local saloon and not tending to the business of passing laws.

California was admitted to the Union on September 9, 1850, and on February 14, 1851, the State Legislature met for their last session in San Jose. The Act of Removal had passed, and the Capitol was relocated to Vallejo, its second, but still only temporary, home. It was later moved to Benicia but there, too, only for a short time. Finally, by an enactment, the Capitol was permanently established in Sacramento.

While the Legislature had been in session in San Jose, the boundaries of Santa Clara County were set. One of them ran along the summit of the Coastal Range, alongside the San Andreas Fault, legally separating Santa Clara from Santa Cruz County for some distance. It was also discovered, after delving into the property situation, that there were few, if any, perfect titles anywhere in the valley or the mountains! Separating the Mexican Land Grants from the public domain, and settling the rights and squabbles of property "owners" took years of concentrated effort by the U.S. Land Commission. But once a claim was finally confirmed, land surveys were made and patents issued thereon, so eventually everyone was satisfied.

CHAPTER 12

LOS GATOS ("THE CATS")

There are many legends surrounding the naming of Los Gatos, originally called Forbes Mill. All are steeped in excitement, and some even in tragedy. Since in the Spanish language, Los Gatos means "The Cats", the most logical reason for the choice, of course, was that wildlife was still plentiful in the mid 1800's. Wildcats of all sizes and descriptions, but most of the stub-tailed bobcat variety, roamed down out of the canyons and were often seen by the local residents.

There are, on record, the following descriptive names attached to various parts of the area long before Los Gatos became a town: Arroyo de Los Gatos (Canyon of the Cats), and La Cuesta de Los Gatos (The Ridge of the Cats).

More heart-wrenching and dramatic stories, however, not based on fact according to William Wulf, were purportedly written by students at Los Gatos High School for their 1919 Yearbook. They have been picked up and enhanced by other authors over the years. Unfortunately, fact and fiction have then become hopelessly entangled. Two of these stories, repeated briefly here, are intended only as a matter of interest for the curious.

One of them tells of the poor shepherd who lost his footing one stormy night as he returned home from tending his flock of sheep in the foothills. He slipped off a narrow footbridge, and plunged into the swollen, rushing waters of Los Gatos Creek. There, he drowned before his helpless and distraught wife could save him.

And, as if that wasn't enough for any woman to bear, the story continues: In the morning, when the young widow went to release the flock from their pen across the creek, she left her baby unattended. Turning back toward her hut, she witnessed her child being snatched from its cradle by marauding wildcats!... "***Los GATOS!***" she screamed.

The poor crazed woman was finally able to make her way on foot to the Santa Clara Mission, some ten miles away. In the quiet sanctuary, she poured out her story of grief and misery to the Padres. Then, so the story concludes, she stumbled back to the site of her once happy adobe hut, and threw herself off the footbridge, accepting the same fate as her unfortunate husband.

The other popular tale depicts a vicious fight between two snarling, spitting wildcats. The drama supposedly was witnessed by a small party of Mexicans and Indians returning from a grueling trip to Santa Cruz. The men had cut their own trail through the tangle of brush, manzanita and poison oak over the mountains and back to the Santa Clara Valley. They came out on a grassy area on one of the northern slopes, and from there had an unobstructed view of the emerald green valley below. It was just the homesite one of the men, Jose Hernandez, had been searching for.

During the ensuing discussion as to whether or not there might be water on the property, a terrible fight between two wildcats started in the nearby brush. Another of the party, Gabriel Serbrian, wanted to shoot the cats. Hernandez, however, wisely restrained him, saying "No! There must be water nearby or there would be no cats." After a two-hour search, the sought-after water was discovered by an old Indian who had accompanied the other men. He claimed he could actually "smell it."

There was a great deal of excitement over the find, and Hernandez exclaimed he would call the site "La Rinconada de Los Gatos" meaning "The Corner of the Cats." It was near the discovery that he built his adobe hacienda.

It is Wulf's contention that brothers-in-law, Jose Hernandez, born in San Jose in 1810, and Sebastian Peralta, born in San Jose in 1790, were quite aware of their surroundings and had extensively explored the Santa Clara Valley. On this particular trip described above they were never lost, never stumbled out of the brush in search of the right piece of land, and never discovered Los Gatos Creek. Hernandez, as a matter of fact, had helped survey a Rancho as early as 1824, and in 1837, belonged to a committee to parcel out the Mission Santa Clara lands to worthy local citizens. It was natural, Wulf continues, that he picked the best for himself. The site was located on the all-important El Camino Real from Mission Santa Cruz to Mission Santa Clara. On July 23, 1839, Jose Hernandez and his co-grantee Peralta filed an "Espediente and Diseno" for El Rancho de Rinconada de Los Gatos to the Mexican Government in Monterey. It was along this important route that Hernandez built his adobe hacienda.

CHAPTER 13

SETTLEMENT OF THE SANTA CRUZ MOUNTAINS

An agreement between Julian Hanks and Isaac Branham, on November 29, 1847, reveals the following:

> *"Know all men by these presents that I, Julian Hanks, of the Pueblo de San Jose, do bargain and sell unto Isaac Branham of the above mentioned place, an equal interest with me in the water and timber privilege for the purpose of erecting a saw mill or other machinery situated on the farm of said Julian Hanks and known by the name of Rancho de Los Gatos, on the road leading from the said Pueblo to Santa Cruz, for the sum of $ 300.00."*

In 1848, after opening and operating a hotel in San Jose known as the "Half Moon", which was situated near the plaza, another interesting character by the name of Zachariah Jones turned his gaze toward the Santa Cruz Mountains. He approached Julian Hanks and Isaac Branham with a business proposition. His idea was to build a dam across Los Gatos Creek, two miles above Los Gatos in the canyon to further develop a saw mill and logging camp.

With Hanks and Branham in accord, Zachariah's next step was to buy the partners out and build a cabin of his own in the area later to be named Lexington. Jones, a devout Methodist, was soon nicknamed "Buffalo" by his neighbors because, in his powerful, thunderous voice he would "quote scriptures to the Lord" as he went about his daily chores. What his neighbors heard reverberating around the canyon, they claimed, was not unlike the sound of a "herd of bellerin' buffalo!"

As white settlers of many nationalities - English, Welch, French, German, Basque, Italian, Bavarian, Portuguese, Irish and Scandinavian - began filtering into the area, they eventually had to confront and contend with the Santa Cruz Mountains. That portion of the Coastal Range was still a looming obstacle between them and the Pacific Ocean. The road to Santa Cruz in those days, was still not much more than a trail used by the Franciscan Fathers.

An excerpt from the diary of one Jerome Paturot, dated September 7, 1850, reads as follows: "The road leading across the Coastal Range was difficult and dangerous to travel as it was infested with bears, wolves and jackals... We learned that it would take fully two days to get there..." (From San Jose to Santa Cruz over the Coastal Range is a distance of approximately 30 miles.)

And from the diary of Levi Stowell, written about the same time, comes the following passage: "I mounted my horse and left for Santa Cruz once more to climb those almost impossible mountains, clambering over rocks and through bushes and sliding down precipices..."

In the following selected excerpts from the Burrell letters and diaries, Mr. Lyman Burrell writes of his mountain homesite in July of 1853: "I selected this ridge where I now live. It seemed a vast, solitary wilderness - no houses and no roads. I knew that bears and lions dwelt here, but I feared them not."

His wife, Clarissa, indicates that the dusty and deeply rutted trail to their "Mountain Home" followed the Los Gatos Canyon to within a short distance of the place where Wrights Station was later located, then up the west side of the canyon to the summit.

"Tis true we came up here with wagons," she wrote her sister on the East Coast, "but we were nearly three days about it... It was very rough and steep, and sometimes very sideling. In some places we found it difficult to keep the cattle from sliding off the lower side."

Apparently, had the Burrells attempted to move their wagons and livestock up from Lexington following the regular route along the ridges and hogbacks, it would have taken them weeks - perhaps even months - of back-breaking labor. So they made use of the logging trail that had been cut in earlier by Hanks, Branham and Jones, which went directly up the canyon instead of skirting it.

In describing the ascent, she wrote, "We came to the foot of the mountains... As we went up higher it grew colder, and long before we got to the top of the mountain, we were surrounded by an ocean of fog. But occasionally, a little wind would blow away the fog when our position would command the most beautiful view of the valley below..."

In later correspondence with her sister and brother, Clarissa wrote, "We have not had the satisfaction of seeing any of the monsters that inhabit these mountains and ravines, in the shape of grizzly bears and panthers, but we see their tracks and know their depredations. One of them came and took a large pig from a pen about a rod from the house. A few nights ago, it came again and attacked a good sized dog that lay by the door."

With so many wild animals making their homes in the thickets and hollow trees, it wasn't long before the Burrell family had a more frightening encounter. Clarissa wrote: "Mr.Burrell (as she referred to her husband, even to close relatives) and Birney (their son) were making a fence along the farther side of the garden. A little before sundown, they heard a great noise among the hogs... Mr. Burrell said he would go up the hill and see what was the disturbance. He jumped over the fence with his ax in his hand and proceeded a few steps up the hill, when he was met by an old grizzly bear and her cub coming down at full speed. He brandished his ax at her, and shouted with all his might to frighten her, but they are an animal that never give even half the road, and it is not safe to wound them if you are within reach, so Mr. Burrell either in turning to let her pass fell, or, she in her haste to go, knocked him over. It was done so quickly he could not tell which. As his feet were towards her she gave him one snap with her teeth on the left limb just above the knee, leaving one large hole on the lower side and two smaller ones on the upper side of it. She then ran three or four steps and turned to look at him. As she saw he did not follow her, she and her cub bounded off down the hill into the brush with all their might."

On March 4th, 1854, Clarissa wrote, "We had some snow here on the mountain... We have plenty of wood around us, both dry and green redwood and oak. The oak burns as well as hickory."

In a paragraph from another letter, Clarissa continued, "Our crops have done much better up here than our fears led us to expect. We have a good supply of wheat, corn, beans, pumpkins, squashes, melons, tomatoes, potatoes, beets, etc., also grape vines, peach trees, and apple trees growing. We continue to like our place very much notwithstanding the wild beasts do continue to live here still."

Perhaps a little wistfully, she added in the conclusion of another of her earthy missives, "The only fault we find with our place is, it is not handy to market."

Lyman was one of the forerunners of the mountain orchardists. At first planting of the fruit trees, he was scoffed at by friends and neighbors alike. No one thought the trees would grow, much less bear fruit, in the altitude, climate and delicate soil always subject to erosion. At first harvest, however, when they were all proved wrong, other orchards began going in across the summit and down the mountain sides.

The Hotel de Redwood (Redwood Lodge), the first hotel in the Summit area, was opened in 1864 on the Old San Jose-Soquel Road, clearly visible ruts and all, 12 miles from Soquel and 4 miles from the Summit. The photograph shown above was taken in 1893. The original hotel, however, burned in 1885 and hence this photograph represents the first rebuilding of the hotel. It burned down again in 1903 and lost its second story during the 1906 San Francisco Earthquake. This facility was again destroyed by fire, rebuilt again and it burned completely before 1930 and it burned down one more time in 1953. Today there is nothing on the property to indicate a hotel ever existed here. Photograph courtesy of Frank Adams.

CHAPTER 14

MOUNTAIN CHARLEY McKIERNAN

Charley McKiernan was an energetic and enterprising Irishman of 23 when he came to the Santa Cruz Mountains in June of 1851. This was three years before the Burrells chose their homesite. According to William Wulf, Charley had the distinction of actually being the "first white settler" in the summit area. There was one other, Captain Harry Love, who lived in the upper Zayante area in the 1830's and operated a small still. Charley, however, chose the summit, with its commanding overviews of both the Monterey Bay to the southwest and the Santa Clara Valley, to the northeast. While primarily engaged in sheep and cattle ranching, Charley also planted many orchards and vineyards over the high slopes. At every opportunity, he increased his holdings and boundaries until eventually he owned 3,000 acres, and a major portion of the Franciscan Trail which passed through it. He was aptly named "Mountain Charley" by his friends and neighbors, but a few of his other noteworthy experiences earned him additional nicknames, as well, such as "Silver Dollar" and "Bad Lamp Charley."

One day, Charley shot and killed a threatening bear, only to discover her two tiny cubs in a nearby thicket. He rescued the furry orphans, and took them back to his cabin where he cared for them for several months. The day he discovered that the two little rascals had an incurable penchant for fresh pig, however, Charley wasted no time in preparing the "most delicious bear stew."

Charley, like his mountain neighbor-to-be, Lyman Burrell, also had more than one encounter with a grizzly. The more famous occasion happened in the spring of 1854. He and his good friend Taylor, rifles in hand, were cruising the woods in search of the wild critters that posed a constant threat to his sheep. The men rounded a bend in a narrow, brush-choked canyon, and came face to face with a giant of a female bear. She reared up on her hind legs to protect her cubs and seemed to tower over the two startled hunters.

Taylor's shot rang out but the bullet only wounded her. Charley's shot, too, missed the mark - a surprise, for he was considered as one of the best marksmen and bear hunters in the mountains. A most dangerous predicament to be in! In the next instant, while Taylor scrambled for the nearest tree, Charley was engulfed in fur. The bear's powerful jaws bore down on the front of his skull, while Charley tried unsuccessfully to whack her a good one on the head with his rifle butt. He did hit hard enough to break the gun, cleanly separating the wooden stock from the barrel. But the enraged bear, undaunted, snapped her mighty jaws shut crushing the area over his left eye.

The struggling Charley went limp in her ferocious grip and his Bowie knife, which he had grabbed after losing the rifle, fell useless to the ground. Taylor watched in horror while the still-snorting bear shook Charley and tossed him aside like a rag doll. Then, methodically, she began raking dried leaves and brush over his body. Leaving him for dead and fortunately forgetting all about Taylor, she ambled off with her cubs.

This rare photograph shows Mountain Charley posing with his wife, the former Barbara Berricke. When this photograph is compared to the portrait of Charley on the opposing page it appears the man is one and the same. A significant mystery! The portrait, by famed artist Andrew P. Hill, was most likely painted from the photograph so Charley would not have to sit for it. It depicts him in a more masculine and outdoor setting, sans wife. The photograph is from the private collection of noted San Jose historian Leonard McKay.

Charles H. McKiernan, Santa Cruz Mountains pioneer and first settler in the summit area, in his most famous pose. He is wearing his wide-brimmed black hat low over his eyes to cover up what he referred to as his "Bad Lamp" - the left eye and forehead badly damaged from his run-in with the Grizzly. Of fiery and determined Irish stock, "Mountain Charley" (as he was called by friends and neighbors) was undoubtedly the most illustrious character in the history of development of the Santa Cruz Mountains, starting in 1851. In the 1860's he married Barbara Berricke, also of Irish descent, and they raised 7 children on their summit ranch, which took in over 3,000 acres of redwood forest.

Although there have been rare recent sightings, the last Grizzly Bear reported to be shot and killed in the Santa Cruz area was in 1889 up on Bonny Doon Ridge.

When the coast was clear, Taylor shinnied down from his perch. He considered it a miracle that Charley, who was in a semi-conscious state, was even breathing at all! With his help and much painful struggling, the two of them made it back to Charley's cabin, where Taylor made him as comfortable as possible for the long hours ahead. Then he took off at a gallop on horseback for San Jose and the nearest medical help.

Wulf, who was able to uncover the actual medical records of the incident, reveals that Taylor enlisted the services of Doctor Bell, who returned with him to the summit area but not until the following morning. Mountain travel at night was simply too hazardous. Although the medical records go into anatomical detail, basically, Doctor Bell found the frontal bone on the injured side of Charley's forehead to be totally crushed. At Charley's insistence, he hurriedly returned to San Jose to fashion a plate of silver, perhaps from pounded Mexican Pesos, to protect the brain. Doctor Ingersoll a colleague returned with Bell to the mountain cabin. Together they again cleaned Charley's wound and installed the plate, noting with some reservations, that it did not quite fit.

A few days later after suffering excruciating headaches and unbelievable pain from the infection that had set in Charley realized that he was in trouble. Taylor assisted in packing him down to San Jose by mule, and it did not take the doctors long to determine that the plate had to be removed with no more delays. Charley, supposedly, while stretched out on a dining room table in the local National Hotel, for lack of better facilities, was the first Californian to undergo surgery with the use of a newly-marketed anesthetic known as Chloroform.

What Charley was left with after the wound finally healed was a badly cocked eye, a disfiguring purple scar, and no bone or plate to protect his brain in that area. From that time on Charley wore a big, wide-brimmed black hat tilted slightly over what he referred to from then on as his "Bad Lamp."

THE ORIGINAL "A - TEAM"

CHAPTER 15

VILLA BRANCIFORTE - THE SMUGGLERS' HIDEOUT

Not all the white settlers came to the Santa Cruz Mountains in the true pioneering spirit. Many were lured to the mineral-and-timber-rich country for the sheer purpose of exploitation and personal gain. There are early accounts of the Indians being coaxed away from the Mission at Santa Cruz by those disreputable characters who then sold them into slavery. And there are equally intriguing tales of hide and tallow smuggling.

Even the ruling Spaniards had found it difficult convincing respectable people to leave their homes in Mexico and establish new ones in the perilous unknown California. So, one of the experimental plans to settle the area at the base of the Coastal Range involved taking a group of ex-convicts, who had no choice, and relocating them at what was called the Pueblo de Branciforte near the Mission Santa Cruz. Unfortunately, the Villa became a hideout for other shady characters and ship jumpers seeking asylum, as well. In its heyday, the smuggling rings and desperadoes, operating out of Branciforte headquarters, stole from the local Mexican Ranchos and sold to foreign interests waiting off shore in their sailing vessels.

The unsavory atmosphere of the Villa hung like a dark and ominous cloud over the Santa Cruz Mission, not too far away. But as the Mission began to lose its control, as all the missions eventually did, strangely enough, so did the Villa. The adobe buildings of the Villa deteriorated, and the Burrells, Schultheis' and Charley McKiernan found the compound to be in a state of ruins in the early 1850's. The outlaws sought an alternative refuge deep within the wooded canyons of the nearby mountains which became notorious in the 1850's and 60's as the new hideout for criminals.

The Frederick Hihn Sawmill at Laurel, on the Santa Cruz side of the mountains, circa 1890. This Mill was one of the best managed and technically advanced in this particular mountain area. From here came a large portion of the lumber that was used to rebuild San Francisco after the Great Earthquake and Fire of 1906.

This photograph is from the Sears' Family collection and appears through the courtesy of William A. Wulf.

CHAPTER 16

LUMBER CAMPS IN THE MOUNTAINS

Roaring lumber camps began to spring up on both sides of the mountains - at Lexington, on the Los Gatos side, and at what is now Boulder Creek, near the headwaters of the San Lorenzo River, on the Santa Cruz side. With little or no regard for the inherent beauty of the area, much less future generations, the "whip sawyers" chewed their way through one stand of redwoods after another. Entire slopes were denuded while opportunistic suppliers shipped thousands upon thousands of board feet of lumber up and down the Pacific Coast.

The newly stimulated public appetite for construction materials seemed insatiable, and the demand for redwood spiraled upward. The price of redwood from the mills in San Jose rose to a staggering $ 100.00 per thousand board feet. "Lumber was exceedingly high," according to a report in THE HISTORY OF SAN JOSE & SURROUNDINGS, "and cost of labor of every kind rose in like proportions."

The loaded flat bed lumber wagons coming down out of the mountains, were pulled by teams of horses and oxen. They were painfully slow, and often subject to "brake failure." Many such ill-fated, out-of-control wagons skidded over cliffs and plunged into the deep ravines below. These splintering accidents were probably what saved the largest and grandest redwoods of them all. As much as they wanted the lumber, the men finally learned their limitations as far as their equipment was concerned.

While the tough burly men furiously worked the double-handled saws, and the dray teams skidded and snaked the logs down the treacherous slopes to the wagon roads below, other teams hauled supplies back up again to the always hungry, hard drinking, often brawling lumbermen.

To help ease the physical pains and mental anguish of so dangerous an occupation, two enterprising young men, Job Dye and Ambrose Tomlinson, set up a distillery. It was located on Zayante Creek, near present-day Felton. The fiery whisky they produced (an important ingredient in making the West so Wild) literally flowed uphill. The "still" owners did a land office business in satisfying the demanding needs of the ever-thirsty loggers.

From the Lexington site, the loggers eagerly supplied the shoring timbers for the further development of the Guadalupe and New Almaden Quicksilver Mines, the very same mines which had originally been developed and worked by the Indians. Quicksilver was still in great demand especially now by the mining industry for use in extracting gold from crushed ore. There were other local construction projects springing up, too, about this time, in the Santa Clara Valley below. Shake and shingle splitters set up their own camps in various mountain locations, while the rugged whip sawyers roamed the wooded areas in pairs around them in search of more and more timber.

Soon these helter-skelter individual enterprises were to be swept into a new era with the advent of the sawmill. In the late 1850's at least three mills were booming on the Santa Cruz side of the mountain. A network of narrow gauge railroad lines were quickly pieced together from Santa Cruz up the canyons to facilitate the moving of the giant redwood logs. On the lumber boom, which followed the Gold Rush, Santa Cruz became the third largest and busiest port along the California coastline. Even Mountain Charley, who had married in the meantime, got into the business. By 1870, he had developed several saw mills on his 3,000 redwood-covered acres to more than amply support his growing family.

CHAPTER 17

EARLY WINE MAKING

Cortez, the conqueror of Mexico, established the wine growing industry for the New World as early as the year 1518. Slowly, it spread northward. One of the most enduring, material gifts given to California by Father Junipero Serra was the small cuttings of grape vines which he brought with him from Baja California. One by one, as the California missions were established and dedicated, Father Serra or his emissaries endowed each with its own private vineyard.

In some areas of California, the vineyards flourished under the right combination of climate and soil. The presiding Fathers at these missions were able to extract an astounding variety of wines from the one basic "Mission Grape" through various simple additive processes. The vineyards grew and spread northward to the Los Angeles basin. For many years, the San Gabriel area was the biggest and best source of mission wine. Then, French immigrant Jean Louis Vignes launched wine commercially about the time the missions were being secularized by the government of Mexico.

In the Santa Clara Valley, the cool Bay air came as a shock to the grape, which was used to a much longer, hotter growing season down in Southern California. This area's day was yet to come, with the introduction of European strains (which later developed into varieties of grapes that thrived on the cooler climate), and with the eventual refinements in the growing and aging process.

In the early days of the missions, wine processing left much to be desired, yet the end result was pleasingly drinkable. The Indians harvested the small supply of mission grapes simply by breaking the clusters off the vines by hand. Then there were others who, barefooted, danced over and over them on the sloping "winery" floor to extract the liquid. The juice from the crushed grape ran into a sump. From the sump it was ladled into large bags made of cowhide, sewn hair-side in, where the fermentation took place. Then the liquid was squeezed through the seam at the bottom of the bags with a hand operated press of two hinged boards.

Since refrigeration was generally unheard of, and storage facilities were at a minimum, presumably the wine was mostly consumed (and enjoyed) as it was processed.

Today, wine making is an agricultural tradition in California. From the humble plantings of the Franciscan Padres at each of the mission sites, and the small vineyards planted in the early 1850's by a handful of Europeans, has emerged an important industry.

More than 140 years ago, a Parisian tailor by the name of Charles LeFranc, settled in the Almaden foothills, east of Los Gatos. After marrying into his neighbor's family, Charles and his new father-in-law, Etienne Thee, joined forces to establish a vineyard. Thee, a farmer by trade and a true master of the soil, took care of the more earthy chores, while LeFranc managed their business affairs.

In 1852, they transported from France, cuttings from some of the finest specimens of varietal vines. (Grapes destined only to be used for wine are referred to as varietals.) Before Thee passed away they also expanded their land holdings, which included property above Saratoga.

About 25 years later, in 1877, history began to repeat itself. This time, a young 18-year-old Frenchman by the name of Paul Masson, was wandering about the vineyards of Charles LeFranc. He was amazed by how much the beautiful area high above Saratoga reminded him of his homeland. The vineyard itself was almost a duplicate of the famous "Cote d'Or" of France's Burgundy Region.

LeFranc was impressed with young Masson's knowledge of wines and growing techniques, and took him on as an employee. Soon they became partners, and for a number of years marketed their wines under the label of "LeFranc & Masson." The partnership blossomed even further when Masson married *his* partner's daughter.

LeFranc and Masson enjoyed total success in their enterprise. The grapes themselves seemed to thrive at the higher altitudes of between 1,400 and 2,000 feet along the northeastern slopes of the Santa Cruz Mountains. They did not seem subject to either frost or mildew. They were even spared the heavy rains which fell predominantly on the higher mountain peaks just to the west.

Following the death of LeFranc, the label was changed to simply read, "Paul Masson." The popularity of the wines and champagnes continued to grow as Masson brought in more and varied cuttings. In addition to the Pinot Noir grape, Masson imported cuttings of the Gamay of Beaujolais, Cabernet Sauvignon, and the white Pinot Chardonnay, Pinot Blanc and Semillon. The Pinot grape took to its new home with gusto, seeming to enjoy the extended summer months for added maturity.

Masson's emphasis was always on quality, not quantity, so he selected his small variety with care. And as always, he combined his Old World methods with the newest techniques and advancements on the market. Many years later, Paul Masson's popular wines and well-known vineyards, modern facilities, and tasting room attained worldwide recognition and numerous awards. According to a brief biographical sketch in the booklet "Ways with Wine": "Perhaps the most satisfying honor of all to this American from Burgundy was when he returned triumphantly to Paris in 1900. His California wines were judged along with the best of the French, and won a distinguished award for quality."

A few miles away, at the Sacred Heart Novitiate, founded by Jesuits exiled from Italy in 1848, more mountain vineyards were planted. They carpeted the sequestered foothills above Los Gatos, just east of the gap. The winery was established very early to help raise funds in support of the Novices who came to study there. Deep within the stone cellars of the monastery, the Fathers' Old World secrets and wine-making talents were put to good use.

For almost 100 years, the Brothers of the Novitiate, under the direction of the Jesuit Fathers, produced altar wines in accordance with the Canon Law of the Catholic Church. These wines were shipped to churches and religious orders all over the United States and various parts of the world.

Although it was a small operation in comparison to other wineries, the Fathers' rather meager beginnings developed into a well equipped laboratory, and a modern plant for bottling and labeling. Over the years, the Fathers acquired more acreage and storage facilities which permitted them to enter the commercial market with a variety of fine wines. They were made with the same patience, care and aging processes as those used for the sacrament.

High in the Santa Cruz Mountains, south of the Summit where the old Soquel-San Jose Road and Morrell Cut Off come together, the Sears family built their ranch which they called "Hazelhurst." Will Sears, who taught at the Highland School, met a young teacher from Burrell School not far away. She was very talented artistically, and also was an accomplished carpenter! Once she and Will were married, she played a major role in the development of the Ranch. She had a hand in the unique floor plan of the house, the water tank house, and the magnificent barn and she even built an aviary next to the house in which to keep a canary. A portable mill was set up on the property so that they could cut their trees and mill their own lumber right on site. The Sears family moved into the house the day prior to the devastating San Francisco Earthquake of 1906, so the story goes. They sought refuge in a large closet while the earth shook and trembled, but immediately thought better of it. A wise decision, as it turned out, as the chimney above that area began to crumble and bricks came crashing through the roof where they had just been standing. The house was jolted off its foundation by the earthquake and major repairs were required. This early 1900s photograph shows a portion of the their attractive house and the well-established orchards. A young child, perhaps the Sears' adopted daughter, Pearl, watches from the porch as a four-horse-power team, hitched to a large water wagon, awaits the command to start sprinkling the road. This was the only method available for controlling the dust on the well-traveled mountain roads during the dry summer months. Photograph, from the Sears' Family collection, appears through the courtesy of William A. Wulf.

CHAPTER 18

EARLY ROADS AND TOLL GATES

In the mid-1850's, with travel on the increase, Mountain Charley McKiernan wasn't long in recognizing the need to develop a feasible route from one side of the Santa Cruz Mountains to the other. He began by clearing and constructing what was to become the first stage route over the Franciscan Trail. He also became one of the partners in the first stage coach line to operate over it. His stop, known naturally as "Mountain Charley's", boasted of his cabin residence which also served as a toll station. Even his own stage company had to pay for the privilege of passing over the section of road that ran through his property.

For some strange reason while collecting tolls at his way station, Charley would occasionally give everyone a thrill. When kids eyed him too curiously from the safety of the coach, he would whip off his hat to reveal the ghastly purple scar beneath. Amid all the terrified squealing and bawling that usually followed, Charley and the drivers would chuckle. Then the ribbons would crack signaling a fast getaway. Perhaps it was due to Charley's fiery Irish temperament, which more than matched his powerful build, but no one ever questioned too loudly or challenged his right to charge the toll or scare the kids!

A little closer to Scott's Valley, still in the area of Bean Creek, Mountain Charley's good neighbor, Charles Martin, also improved the road through his property and established yet another toll station. One day, Martin came face to face with Hannah Carver, who, still unbeknownst to either of them, was about to become his wife. At the moment, however, she was only prepared to pay her toll for the right of passage. Hannah initially mistook Charley for an Indian because of his deeply tanned, weather-beaten complexion! But from this brief encounter romance followed.

Charley Martin, according to his great-granddaughter, Margaret Koch, in her book entitled SANTA CRUZ COUNTY, PARADE OF THE PAST, began buying up land in the Santa Cruz Mountains which adjoined that of McKiernan's. The nest egg he had tucked away after his profitable trip to the Mother Lode country got him started. The money, incidentally, came not from the digging of gold, but from his selling fresh hogs to the hungry miners. The Chinese laborers, in particular, liked to see Martin driving his herd into their camps, as their diet consisted mostly of rice, and boiled pork when they could get it.

The area near where the Martin property adjoined McKiernan's, along Bean Creek, was yet unnamed. "How does Martinville sound?" Charley asked Hannah (or perhaps it was some other well-meaning relative). She smiled demurely, looking over their beautiful meadow surrounded by firs and redwoods, and suggested that "Glenwood" might sound more attractive...

Another of the early road building pioneers was Zachariah "Buffalo" Jones. With his saw mill and logging camp doing a good business at the headwaters of Los Gatos Creek, he claimed as much land and as many stands of redwood as he could with squatter's rights across his so-called private property. But the logging road he put in (such as it was with its deep ruts, steep grades and dangerous turns) remained in deplorable condition. He hoped to convince the Santa Clara County Board of Supervisors to improve it for him.

In 1854, the Supervisors sent out a party of explorers to examine the situation. In charge of the expedition was Sheriff John Murphy, an expert horseman of derring-do. He had heard of a certain Mrs. Farnham who had made it over the mountains in a sulky - alone!

Historian William Wulf, however, found evidence in his research that Mrs. Farnham, probably unbeknownst to Sheriff Murphy, had a little help from an employee - an Irish man-servant, - of some physical strength. And the vehicle behind the horse was not a sulky but a small wooden cart. The two of them did traverse the mountains, from Santa Cruz on her way to a business meeting in San Francisco. (This was the same Mrs. Eliza W. Farnham, Wulf points out, who had earlier transported those American Beauties from the East Coast to the West.) She rode where the dirt trail was passable, and her man-servant fought the extremely hazardous terrain, especially down the north face, on foot. In some places where the trail narrowed dangerously, they had to remove the wheels, which Mrs. Farnham rolled separately while her "mechanic" picked up the cart and carried it on his back!

Still, not to be outdone, especially by a woman, Sheriff Murphy was determined to make it over the mountains to the coast and back with a favorable report.

When they reached the summit area, Murphy and his party were delighted to discover that so much had already been accomplished on the road beyond that point. What was considered the most difficult, steep and winding mountain area had already been cleared and widened, thanks to the combined efforts of the two Charleys - McKiernan and Martin.

On his return to San Jose, Murphy claimed it would cost only $ 10,000 to construct a road from Zachariah Jones' place to the Santa Cruz County line at the summit, a distance of about eight miles.

According to William Wulf in a newspaper article, Jones continued to pester and petition the County Board of Supervisors to make improvements on his primitive logging road. Instead, on April 20, 1853, the State of California approved the Plank and Turnpike Road Act, which put the need for Jones' road in jeopardy altogether. Then the County Board of Supervisors seemed to quietly back away from the issue. Over the next few years, an irate Jones caused as much trouble - in the form of charges, counter charges, and other litigations - as the formidable mountains posed themselves to the road engineers who were about to tackle them. Over Jones' protests, the time seemed right for the construction of a new toll road by private enterprise. The Santa Cruz Gap Turnpike Joint Stock Company was formed early in 1857, according to Wulf, and at its final meeting on December 19th of that same year, "a survey was adopted to construct a road from 12 to 20 feet wide from the toll house" (this one located in Los Gatos, at the entrance to the gap), "up the west side of the Los Gatos Creek Canyon through the lands of Zachariah Jones to the Santa Clara County line at the summit of the Santa Cruz Mountains."

Jones filed suit against the Turnpike Company. But while he continued to fuss and fume over the bypassing of his wagon road, and the commandeering of his other lands for the new road, workcrews began the arduous tasks of improving the old Franciscan Trail.

The grades of the new road to, through, and out of the Lexington area were relatively easy, but approaching the summit, they were steep and treacherous. The dirt trail, in many instances, hugged the sides of sheer cliffs, and tampering with it was dangerous business. The workmen chopped, cut, and cleared away trees, chaparral and poison oak (which gave the workmen fits), while horses worked in pairs with heavy wooden drags behind them.

Although the Franciscan Trail was the primary route to the coast, there were many tributaries leading off down canyons and along ridges which were also pioneered in the late 1850's and early 60's - the Bear Creek, Summit, Glenwood, Laurel and Soquel Roads, to name a few. And leading up and out of the little logging community of Saratoga, over an even more hair-raising route, was the "Saratoga and Pescadero Turnpike and Wagon Road", the forerunner of State Highway 9.

During these years of formative growth and major, dramatic changes in the West, powerful Chinese syndicates supplied many of the workmen to do the backbreaking labor. In particular, it was Chinese labor that helped build the road system through the High Sierra and also the Santa Cruz Mountains. The Chinese also dug tunnels, cut timbers, laid track, and made charcoal to run the smelters, etc., work that no one else was anxious to do.

Paradoxically, Euro-Americans felt threatened by these Oriental immigrants who were becoming part of the work force. There were other justifiable reasons for animosity besides the threat to job security. Many immigrants were arriving with contagious diseases and, due to a lack of water and sanitation and medical help at the work sites, the spread of disease could not be stemmed easily. Also, opium seemed to be a readily available commodity amongst the Chinese workers, and it was openly offered for sale. Historical accounts indicate many instances of anti-Chinese violence wherever Chinese lived or congregated in groups, and unions protecting the white worker began to flex their muscles.

Traditionally, the Chinese kept to themselves, setting up their own work camps away from the Caucasians. One such group in Nevada finally had "had it" with the discrimination and violence and decided to quit the work area entirely near Tybo, a mining community. The unionists were so smugly pleased that they passed the hat and helped pay the stage fare to get the Chinese out and back where they came from. The Chinese were imposed upon and maligned. Nevertheless, today they are credited with accomplishing much of the pioneering construction work in the West.

But, meanwhile, back at the gap, on May 5, 1858, Joseph Johnson and Peter Davidson doled out the first toll levied on the new turnpike. The tolls that poured in over the next few months, however, were hardly enough to cover the damage caused by the severe winter storms to come. Relentlessly, one after another, the rain-laden weather fronts bore down on the California coast out of the Pacific and Gulf of Alaska. Floods, and the resulting rock slides, caused more havoc that first winter than it cost to put the road in initially.

An early newspaper account indicates what surrounding conditions were probably like, as crews worked feverishly to keep the road open to mountain travelers: "More than six feet of rain has fallen in these mountains, and streams have swollen so tremendously in consequence that trees along the banks were uprooted, fences and sheds washed away, and deep inroads made into bordering ranches."

Besides devastating the road, the storms took some of the vinegar out of "Buffalo" Jones, as well. Even though he had been awarded $ 500 by the courts in his suit against the Turnpike Company, he finally tired of the legal hassles he himself had created. Deciding to retire, he sold his property to John Pennell Henning, who is now credited with being the actual "founder" of the community of Lexington. Henning named the area the "City of Lexington" after his former hometown in Missouri, and did much of the original surveying and subdividing of the land. For the next twenty years, according to William Wulf, Lexington, with its important Way Station, was the "largest settlement in the Redwood District."

In 1867, James Kennedy and his wife built a home at the southern limits of Los Gatos. For the next ten years, their residence also served as the Santa Cruz Gap and Turnpike Company Toll House. However, after the Toll Company Charter expired on November 16, 1877, according to Wulf, the high tolls (and in some cases unreasonable double tolls where two wagons in tandem were pulled by one team of horses) remained in effect. Irate teamsters tore down the toll gate, dragged it to the Main Street Bridge, and threw it into the creek! The gate was replaced a few days later, only to be torn down for the second time!

Wulf continues, at this point, "The Turnpike Company obtained a court order enjoining the men (teamsters) from further use of the road without paying a toll. Furthermore, they were ordered to pay for using the road while the gate was down. They were also fined $ 25.00 for each infraction."

Then, on January 28, 1878, D. B. Moody, secretary of the Toll Company, accompanied by others, erected yet another toll gate. Teamsters stood by quietly and watched the proceedings. "When the gate was in position, Mr. Moody ordered Mr. Kennedy to collect the first toll. At this point, the teamsters rushed the gate, tore it off and threw it over the bank, with Mr. Moody holding on firmly."

The gate was never replaced. The then-700 residents of the Redwood District, petitioned that the road be declared a public highway, and the Santa Clara County Board of Supervisors agreed. The Board determined that the Corporation had been liberally rewarded for its initial $ 7,000.00 investment. Over 20 years, the Corporation had collected $ 137,127.91 in tolls, and paid the stockholders $ 52,659.50 in dividends.

CHAPTER 19

SPANISH INFLUENCE ON FOOD

In studying the area today, there are many reminders of the past. Because the Mexican and Spanish customs were not only retained but actually encouraged and nurtured as well, their influence has remained quite strong. According to accounts in THE HISTORY OF SANTA CLARA COUNTY, however, in the mid-1800's, the native way of life was not all that easy for the newly arriving Americans to understand.

Some of the Spanish people were very stylish, and the ladies wore rich silks with intricate embroidery work. Their long, low ranch-style adobe haciendas were also richly adorned with expensive carpeting and lavish draperies. And they loved to entertain!

Many of the Americans, no matter how often they joined in the festive occasions, entertainment's, and party-goings, still found the customs and eating habits odd. One delightful American lady, "Grandma" Bascom, as she was referred to, operated a San Jose boarding house. She described an elegant wedding, between a certain Miss Pico and a Mr. Campbell, that was held in one of the most fashionable adobe mansions: "It was very grand, but the odd dresses and the odd dishes upset my gravity more than once."

On another occasion, she baked a special 6-egg cake to be served at a party she, herself, was hosting:

"I made an elegant cake," she sighed, *"which I was going to pass around in fine style. I began by passing it to one of the Spanish ladies, and she took the whole cake at one swoop, wrapped it up in the skirt of her gorgeous silk dress and said, 'Muchas gracias!' (Thank you very much!). I never was so surprised in my life but there was nothing I could do. The rest of us had to go without cake that time."*

Over the past one hundred years, many other exotic, ethnic foods have been introduced into the California cuisine - Chinese, Japanese, Thai, Indonesian, Greek, etc. But it is the influence of the Mexican and Spanish with which Californians started that continues to predominate.

In Jane Butel's HOTTER THAN HELL cookbook, she explains that "Over 7,000 varieties of chiles grow throughout the world, differing greatly in size and ranging in flavor from pleasantly spicy to downright satanic." Quite a few varieties are grown in California like the hybrid Anaheim Chile, and the flavorful mild Bells in a variety of colors - red, green, yellow, and purple. The Jalapeno from Mexico is fiery, as is the dried Szechwan from China. They are often relied on to spice up any California dish.

It has not been easy. All this acquired taste has taken Californians years to conquer. And visitors to California, even today, may find *their* gravity upset more than once.

In an early newspaper account, a rather elegant dinner, hosted by Mexican dignitaries for a large party of Americans, revealed the following menu:

Caldo Mexicano

Ensala   Frijoles   Tortillas

Puchero

Mole' de Guajolote

Tamales

Stewed Veal Stuffed with Almonds

Chili Tiero

Frutas

Pulque   Chocolate

The Caldo Mexicano turned out to be a soup more like the drippings from roast beef. As the Americans, politely observant recalled, "The proper way to get rid of the soup was to drink it." The Mexican hosts did. The American guests did not. They simply smelled it and smiled faintly... In further explaining the menu, the article described the Ensala as being a salad of fresh lettuce spread thickly with sweet oil, onions and garlic. The Frijoles were the traditional Mexican beans, and the Tortillas were, of course, the thin rounds of flatbread.

The entree consisted of Arroz Seco, boiled rice mixed with carrots and hard boiled eggs; Puchero, which turned out to be a form of Mexican "Irish Stew" - a tasty combination of fried cabbage, carrots and goatmeat; and the Mole' de Guajolote, a kind of turkey fricassee with vegetable gravy, hot fat and red peppers. When it came to the Mole', the article goes on, the Americans who ate the gravy asked for ice to soothe their burning tongues. The Mexicans, on the other hand, ate the gravy with a relish, even dipping their bread in it. Then, there were also Tamales, or Mexican Croquettes, which, for that particular meal, were made of a raisin, nut and fruit combination, rolled in corn meal and boiled in corn husks.

The Chili Tiero consisted of green peppers, stuffed with chopped chicken and raisins, which were dipped in a batter and fried in hot lard. Probably the only dish on the menu that could successfully be downed by the Americans without causing a lot of tongue fanning and wiping of tears, was the veal stuffed with almonds.

For dessert there were fresh fruits in season, and to wash the whole meal down, Chocolate for the faint-hearted, and Pulque which was served to the guests in small wine glasses. Pulque is a form of Mexican wine made from the milky juice of the Manguey, a species of the century plant. It was to the Mexican what Bock beer was to the German, and it was reported that a Mexican could drink 4 quarts of it without becoming intoxicated. For the Americans, however, the taste of the wine was compared to that of diluted yeast.

> *From Chapter 15 of TWO YEARS BEFORE THE MAST by Richard Henry Dana, Jr.:*
> *"Frijoles - the perpetual food of the Californians, but which, when well cooked, are the best beans in the world."*

A Concord Coach drawn by a four-horse team. The open windows exposed travelers to rain, snow, and clouds of dust as well as chewing tobacco from the driver.

According to Wells Fargo history, "The man who held the ribbons and cracked the whip over a six-horse team was, in the late 1850's and '60's, often more highly esteemed than the millionaire or statesman who rode behind him." Equally important was the man who rode along side him! He was armed with a Company issued double-barrel shotgun, and a pocket pistol designed by Colt for good measure, to protect the cargo and lives of the passengers. From the Log Book of George L. Colgrove, who drove such a stage: "A party of 12 rented the Concord Coach for a trip to Santa Cruz - seven men and five women. Six sat outside and six were inside. It made the coach a little bit top-heavy and I had to drive cautiously around the turns."

CHAPTER 20

STAGE LINES TO SANTA CRUZ

In November 1861, according to a news release in the San Jose Mercury Herald, oil was discovered by Joseph Smith in the hills near Lexington. It appeared to be of very high quality, and of an "inexhaustible supply." A little later that same month, the Swain Brothers discovered cinnabar at the entrance to the canyon at Lexington, and there was another oil strike, not far away, near Moody's Gulch, "about one hundred rods from the Santa Cruz Road." There were other intriguing rumors, too, (mostly hushed) of gold mines in the Santa Cruz Mountains rich with nuggets.

Nourished by the age-old promise to "get rich quick", a strange lot of people began to flock to the area. Some came to the over-endowed mountains in search of wealth, others came to the foothills in search of their health.

With the stage route open, little towns and resorts began to pop up and flourish like California wild flowers. Some of the mountain residents generously offered their bedrooms to weary travelers until they realized that mountain travel was no passing fancy. The late Walter Young, long-time resident of Los Gatos, who grew up in the Santa Cruz Mountains, explained in his memoirs how many of the mountain hotels came into being. When travelers would ask for a night's lodging, the obliging farmer with the big house was happy to accommodate them. But in some cases, these late night drop-in's became too much of a good thing. In self defense, the mountain residents began charging a fee for room and board.

* * * Advertisement * * *

PIONEER STAGE LINE

From Santa Clara to Los Gatos, Lexington and Way Stations

The Finest Mountain Scenery and the Best Mountain

Road in the State by this route. The Coaches are

Driven by Old and Experienced Drivers.

Fare $ 2.50

Ward & Colgrove....Proprietors

The Pioneer Stage Line from Santa Clara to Santa Cruz used exclusively Concord Coaches for carrying passengers. The Concord Coach was a top-of-the-line stagecoach built by the Abbot-Downing Company of Concord, New Hampshire. What made it so "luxurious" were the two leather straps running lengthwise upon which the body of the coach rested. These "shock absorbers" helped take some inequities - but not all - out of the dirt roads. The coach weighed 2,500 pounds, and cost $ 1,250. Not a bad buy at 50 cents a pound!

Entry from the Log Book of George L. Colgrove, Pioneer Stagecoach Driver and Operator, July 15, 1869: "We started out with the stage from San Jose and did the regular business. We did the regular routine and got up to Lexington and changed horses and got dinner. From there we had the six-horse team over the Santa Cruz Mountains to Scotts Valley. There we changed to a four-horse team into Santa Cruz."

The run over the mountains, in spite of the Pioneer Stage Line's attractive ad, was long, steep, winding, and perilous. Although continuous attempts were made to smooth out and widen the gritty trail, rarely was it wide enough for one vehicle to safely pass another. And the steep grades, coupled with the gusty, unpredictable canyon winds, made 'gearing up and down' with the use of real horse power, a necessity.

Often times, the stage would meet a logging train pulled by eight to ten oxen. The oxen wore enough bells to be heard quite a distance, usually offering the stage drivers time to pull over as close to the bank as possible to allow the logging team to pass. But this was still scary business, as the suddenly skitterish thoroughbred horses, and the dull plodding oxen were never on the best of terms.

"Whoa....WHOA....Easy boy...." the stage drivers would holler down to the restless teams trying to keep them calm. Leather whips of authority crackled and snapped in the tense air.

On one particular trip, the stage came face to face with a lumbering bakery wagon on a dangerous curve. As the team of snorting horses rapidly approached, the bakery driver became confused and panicky. "What should I DO?" he cried in fright.

"Well," came a little boy's voice from inside the stagecoach, "to start with, why don't you get back *up* on your wagon?!"

According to Colgrove, it was "pretty risky" to take anyone on as a driver who was not experienced and familiar with the road.

Colgrove's stage operation out of San Jose bound for the coast came into direct competition with Mountain Charley's already established Santa Cruz Stage Company coming from the opposite direction. Cutthroating between the two concerns occasionally reduced the coach fare from $ 2.50 to $ 1.00 a head. What with drivers' wages to pay, horses to feed and quarter, and tolls to pay at several locations along the route, profits were very slim, indeed!

At one point in time, when forced into an uncomfortable financial bind, the Pioneer Stage Line decided to use an alternate route to Santa Cruz, bypassing Mountain Charley's altogether. This would eliminate two tolls, at McKiernan's and Martin's, from the daily expenses.

The fork in the road was located at Patchen, a tiny but important mountain community located a mile or so from the summit on the Santa Clara Valley side of the grade. Here was located the United States Post Office servicing the mountain area. When Colgrove first inspected the route, he was disappointed to find it impassable in some sections closer to the town of Soquel due to neglect and the ravages of past winter storms. But with the help of some of the local residents, he was able to clear and repair the route just enough so that his stagecoach could squeak through. It was actually three miles longer to Santa Cruz via Soquel, but Colgrove's customers seemed not to mind the inconvenience or the rougher of the two stage routes, and once again the business picked up.

Several months went by before Mountain Charley would admit it was his turn to feel the financial pinch. He came forward with a plan to merge the two stage companies. Although Colgrove was basically against the idea, the consolidation was effected and a daily line was established. The passenger fare was once again set at $ 2.50.

Colgrove Takes a Break...

It wasn't long before Colgrove, now acting as driver, found himself out of a job with the new stage company. It was during this period of unemployment that he decided to get together a small camping party for lack of anything better to do. He and several of his good friends loaded their bedrolls, a supply of grub and a five-gallon jug of whisky on an eight-passenger wagon, and pointed their team of horses toward the Santa Cruz Mountains.

On their first afternoon out, the men camped across the road from the Ferguson Ranch above Saratoga. Before sundown, they had all caught a mess of trout in King's Creek, and shot some dove in the meadow. Prepared over an open fire, the day's catch provided a fine supper. Then the tired hunters spread out their bedrolls under the trees, fully anticipating a good night's sleep. But it was a restless night for all of them as they listened to the cacophony of strange and unnerving forest sounds.

The next day, the red-eyed men went off once again on their hunting and fishing expeditions only to return to a mystery back at camp. When one of them reached under the wagon seat for the five-gallon jug of whisky, with which they all had hoped to promote a sounder night's sleep, they discovered the storage space empty!

Angry and frustrated, the men marched across the road and down to the Ferguson ranch house. The Ferguson brothers said they were aware of their presence in the vicinity when they heard shots and then noticed the campfire later in the evening. They also said that they had seen no one nosing around the camp site while it had been unoccupied. "However," one of the brothers continued, "there is an old codger named Swift living in a nearby cabin who has a terrible penchant for whisky. If there's any in the vicinity..." his voice trailed off. "Of course, not meanin' to accuse him, or anything, as he's an agreeable enough neighbor..."

The Ferguson Brothers politely declined the invitation to accompany the campers on their search, and so Colgrove and his friends took off alone in the direction that had been pointed out to them. Cautiously, they approached the cabin where they found the bewhiskered Swift dead-drunk in his bunk. When the men shook him awake, he at first feigned complete surprise at their accusation, and then alternated between absolute flat denials and tears of remorse. The men let him slip back into his drunken stupor, and continued their relentless search. Out in back of the cabin, deep within a hollow redwood stump, the mystery ended. There was their precious demi-john, nearly empty!

With the better part of their whisky gone, the men decided to head for Santa Cruz and, hopefully, a better time. They broke camp and took off, not anxious to spend another sleepless night in the company of wild beasts and the whispering, sighing redwoods. Traveling by moonlight took more time and caution than usual, but by early dawn, they approached their destination. As they came along the San Lorenzo River, the sweet, pungent aroma of freshly baked breads, sticky buns, pies and cookies wafted through the crisp morning air. A baker-friend of Colgrove lived nearby, and Colgrove surprised his famished companions by turning the wagon in through the gate posts. The good-natured baker supplied the men with samplings of his most tasty delicacies. Colgrove, in his diary, recalled the sheer pleasure of laying out on the banks of the river as the sun came up, and enjoying the mouth-watering slabs of hot mince-meat pie.

The men decided to make the trip complete by going down to the beach at Santa Cruz before starting the long trek back over the mountains. As they approached the shore, they were treated to a rare and spectacular sight. Millions of sardines had lured mackerel, in hot pursuit, right up into the shallow, foamy waters and onto the beach itself! As the news spread rapidly through town, men, women and children alike came running across the sands to scoop the trapped fish up in their arms.

Colgrove and his companions, in spite of the competition, literally filled their wagon with the slippery, flopping fish. They found some hay to pack around their prize and then decided to head for home immediately before there was any spoilage. They gave up another night's sleep to travel under the light of the moon, and the next morning were wearily but happily hawking their mackerel to the merchants of San Jose right off the back of their wagon.

CHAPTER 21

TALES OF THE BANDITOS

Lawlessness continued to flourish in the Santa Cruz Mountains, especially a little further south in the Gabilans at the site of the Quicksilver Mines. Here, two magnificent mountain peaks stood like guardian sentinels but they could not stop the outlaws who holed up in New Almaden. Few were ever caught, much less brought to trial. An account in the HISTORY OF SANTA CLARA COUNTY reveals the following:

"In those earlier days, the social conditions of the workmen, who were mostly Mexicans, was inferior. The place was noted for lawlessness and was a rendezvous for Mexican banditti. Little restraint was exercised over the men, and gambling, drinking and other excesses were common. Large wages were paid and it was no uncommon occurrence for a man to be killed after each pay day..."

Bandits and highwaymen preyed on the mountain residents and the wayfaring stranger, as well. On the 640-acre Schultheis' Ranch, "Susan Schultheis was accosted one day by three heavily armed men, and forced to cook a meal for them." The bandits hungrily devoured the food put before them and then took off in a cloud of dust with the sheriff and his posse hot on their heals for "murders that had been committed."

The suspects, thought to be Sidneyites (criminals deported from their own homeland of Australia), were now busily terrorizing the San Francisco Bay area. The men were overtaken somewhere along the Laurel or Glenwood Canyons, according to one report, shot on sight by the posse, and dumped unceremoniously alongside the road.

Another fierce bandido, whose reputation for spilling blood almost equaled that of Joaquin Murrietta, was the dashing and handsome Tiburcio Vasquez. His entire life seemed to be one long series of violent crimes committed around the state. His record for eluding the authorities, escaping death, and sweeping the ladies off their feet was excellent, however.

One of the boldest crimes he ever committed, in the company of his four cohorts, took place in the quiet little town of Tres Pinos, south of San Jose, near Hollister. Here the bandidos robbed and plundered the general store, hotel and private residences, killing three hapless victims and seriously wounding a small boy in the doing. Then they stole the horses from the hotel stable on which to pack off their booty.

Another daring crime attributed to Vasquez was the cold-blooded murder of two miners just returned from the Mother Lode country. There was a particular ranch in Los Gatos whose hosts offered welcomed lodging to a continuous stream of gold seekers. One evening, while two of them were preparing to stop for the night, a group of bandits - reportedly with the feared Vasquez in their midst - suddenly rode up into the courtyard on their snorting, wild-eyed horses. With little formality, they shot the miners and made off with their gold.

Vasquez continued to raid and plunder his way through California, and posse after posse took the field against him without success. In the mountains Vasquez felt safe, and he maintained hiding places up an down the Coastal Range from Los Angeles to Santa Cruz. Equaling or even surpassing his growing number of enemies, however, were his loyal and ever-vigilant friends living along the routes. They cared for him, loved him (on more than one occasion), and kept him well informed of the movements of the law officers never far behind.

One night, Vasquez had the audacity to rendezvous with one of his favorite senoritas at a public dance in Hollister. When the posse closed in they only caught a glimpse of what they thought was an agile young woman, in full skirt, darting across the road, leaping onto a horse and galloping off into the night. For Vasquez, some senoritas would give up anything... even their dancing clothes!

Vasquez was eventually shot and forced to surrender near Los Angeles. He was transported, imprisoned, accused, convicted and sentenced to hang for his crimes in San Jose, California. His last request before execution, according to James D. Horan in his book THE AUTHENTIC WILD WEST, was to "see his coffin." It was brought to his cell. He admired the satin lining while chewing on a cigar, and then exclaimed: "Si'...I can sleep here forever very well!" Much to the relief of the general populace, but remorse of his faithful senoritas, Vasquez, according to author Dennis McLoughlin in his book, WILD & WOOLLY, "did his last tango on the gallows" in San Jose on March 19, 1875.

"Some of the girls, on the sly would even dance if they had a chance and the wickedest of boys and young men would play Euchre (a card game played with a diminished deck) for nails on rainy days at the carpenter's shop."

CHAPTER 22

STAGE ROBBERS

The log book of George L. Colgrove reveals that in the spring of 1874, after he had finally re-established himself in the stage company business, another fugitive was on the loose in the Santa Cruz Mountains.

"It was Ward's (his partner) day out of San Jose. In backing his wagon out of the barn to turn it around, he got his foot under the wheel and mashed his big toe pretty badly. He couldn't go out that day so he had to rustle around to find someone who had some idea of the road. It was pretty risky to take anyone that was not acquainted with it," a fact that had already been established.

A relief driver, by the name of John Pursly Smith, was finally located and agreed to make the run over the mountains to Santa Cruz.

About half way between Alma and Wrights, a robber by the name of Albert P. Hamilton, known more simply by just his last name, jumped out from behind a big redwood tree as the stage approached. He pointed a double-barreled shotgun at the surprised driver, hollering for him to stop. Then he demanded the express box, which the stage was not carrying, and the mail sack bound for the Post Office at Patchen. Momentarily disappointed, Hamilton threw the sack on the ground and gave it a swift kick in disgust before handing it back. Then, addressing the passengers inside, and the two or three riding atop the stage, he ordered them to throw down their money and valuables.

Altogether, Hamilton got away with about eighty dollars and a silver watch, the only prized possession of an immigrant who was about to make his new home in the Santa Cruz Mountains.

In late April of the same year, another robbery occurred in the vicinity of a giant redwood tree near Glenwood. This time, Hamilton was operating with a partner.

The sheriffs of both Santa Clara and Santa Cruz Counties feared that any more such incidents or bad publicity would keep people from traveling, so Sheriff Bob Orton of Santa Cruz came up with a plan. Each route over the mountains was to be covered that very night by deputies posing as passengers, and all the posses were then to report back to Patchen at the conclusion of the dragnet operation.

"Carry arms and be on the lookout," were his orders. Colgrove's entry indicated that "Everyone was tickled to go!"

Colgrove personally drove the stage on this particular night, and was assigned to cover the regular route, which was the shortest. He and the other deputies got up to Mountain Charley's about 11:00 P.M. Charley's toll gate (always set up to keep people from sneaking through to avoid the toll at odd hours) was securely in place. The deputies decided not to arouse and involve Charley (an unfortunate decision for them in the long run), and most carefully moved the pole which extended across the road. They quietly proceeded through with the horses and stage, unnoticed.

Later, back at Patchen, three groups of deputies (one was still out) converged with nothing more to report than a rumor that "someone had seen two men with shotguns going up Los Gatos Creek." Thirsting for action, the combined group of deputies tore down the mountain to a woodchopper's camp where the suspicious characters had supposedly been sighted.

Here the posse was offered a bite to eat while they rested briefly. Then they set out again, up the canyon in hot pursuit. Opposite Wrights place, the road gave out, so the men hitched the teams of horses and took off again on foot.

The men came upon a little cabin, and in their eagerness, pounced upon the poor occupant as he stepped out his front door. Innocent though he was, the posse made him lead the way back to Patchen to be properly identified. It was there they learned the bitter-sweet news that Hamilton, along with his partner, had already been captured - by the posse from Saratoga and with the help of none other than Mountain Charley himself!

Charley, as a matter of fact, was actually the first to see the culprits hours earlier as he was dressing out a deer not far from his cabin. He hallooed to them in a friendly manner thinking at first they were neighbors. But when he got no response, and noted that the two men high-tailed it off down a little trail toward Bean Creek, Charley was pretty certain that something was afoot. Later, when the posse that had come up from Saratoga stopped by for a little informative chat, Charley confirmed his suspicions out loud. He led the posse down the trail to an abandoned farmhouse.

As the lawmen began to surround the place, rifle shots broke the silence. The redwood forest suddenly seemed to come alive with the rustlings and scurryings of a thousand furry, feathered creatures. Another volley of shots rang out, and in the momentary confusion, Charley gained access to the house. One of the surprised men made a move to raise his rifle but Charley was ready. He shot and slightly wounded both of them.

On the way to jail, Hamilton is said to have sneered at the deputies from Saratoga, "A hell of a lot of heroes you are! I would like to be turned loose and I would make short work of you. That cockeyed fellow with the rifle was the only one I was afraid of!"

Hamilton was sent to prison for 10 years, but after only 8 months' incarceration, he managed to escape by cutting the lock on his cell. At the same time, he also released two convicted murderers, and the three escapees vanished into the night. A $200 reward was posted, and

Mountain Charley was considerably uneasy for the safety of his family until news came of Hamilton's recapture, although Hamilton swore he never returned to the Santa Cruz Mountains as he had threatened to do.

George B. Smythe, lone highwayman in 1881, was originally a school teacher who "fell from grace." He held the record for robbing 11 stage coaches single-handedly within a three week period. He was finally caught in a miner's cabin in Guadalupe, out near the quicksilver mines.

But it was Black Bart who was the real enigma of the stage line. He, also single-handedly, robbed 28 stages over a 10-year period. For some unknown, egotistical reason, he enjoyed leaving bits and pieces of original poetry (most often filled with misspelled words) at the scene of each robbery, taunting and frustrating one sheriff and inspector after another.

A strong box bolted to the floor of a stage coach proved to be Black Bart's undoing. He found he could not rifle the box and keep his eye and gun on the irate driver at the same time, and received a bullet to prove it. He got away, but it wasn't long before he was apprehended in San Francisco in 1883 by a Wells Fargo Chief of Detectives, James B. Hume, who traced him through a laundry mark on his handkerchief inadvertently dropped at the scene of the crime! He should have stuck to poetry.

Strangely enough it was discovered that Black Bart had been leading a double life. In the city, under the name of Charles Bolton, he was well-liked and highly respected. His split personality did not save him from prison, however, and he spent several years in San Quentin for his crime spree. When he was finally released, he simply faded into anonymity and was never heard from again.

Mr. Crane, 1892
owner of Adolph Rapp Sr. Ranch

Catherine McAlpine Crane, 1889

J.C. Rankin
Beau Brummell of Highland-189

Bertha Hadsell - age 15

The Good Doctor Goldman

Anna Hadsell - age 16 in 1891

H.S. Maynard, Sr. Family

Early Mountain Settlers
Courtesy of Frank Adams

CHAPTER 23

ANOTHER CHARLEY OF NOTE

There was another Charley in the Santa Cruz Mountains - a stage driver by the full name of "Six-horse Charley Parkhurst", also known as "One-Eyed Charley", (from being kicked in the face by a horse), who had the run from Watsonville to Santa Cruz. Coincidentally, this Charley also wore a "sinister black patch" over one eye, and was considered to be one of the "toughest, orneryest, spittinest, drinkinest, cussinest" drivers of the lot.

No one ever thought twice, for obvious reasons, of Charley's elaborate hand-embroidered buckskin gloves, worn constantly, which eventually turned out to conceal rather small, delicate hands. Only after death, in a lonely cabin near the community of Soquel, was Charley's well-kept secret revealed. The driver of those six snorting, wild-eyed mustangs, who for years snaked a reeling stagecoach over impossible roads and through all kinds of weather, turned out to be a woman!

Charley's partner, Frank Woodward who had sat beside her for years, could not believe what the Coroner was saying. Why, Charlotte, Charlotte, Charlotte!

Another interesting note about Charley Parkhurst was that "his" name appeared in the great register of voters in the County of Santa Cruz in 1866. Apparently Charley actually voted in the election of November 3rd, 1868, long before women had the right to do so.

Santa Cruz Stage Terminus, circa 1866.

A Concord Stage, drawn by four horses, sits in front of the popular Pacific Ocean House Hotel located on Pacific Avenue in Santa Cruz. This is the only known photograph of a stagecoach which had just traversed the Santa Cruz Mountains, and is presented here through the courtesy of William A. Wulf.

CHAPTER 24

A RAILROAD COMPANY EMERGES

"The Sense of the Seventies" describes what it was like in California 125 years ago: At the end of the Civil War, the West began to feel the post-war boom. With no more Confederate Raiders to stand off, or forts to build, contractors and ex-military men drifted west in search of profitable employment. Since California was operating on a hard-cash economy, the situation was even more enticing. Suddenly there was a surge in demand for goods that began to stimulate manufacturing. This economy soon resulted in a period of intense development. San Francisco, Sacramento and Los Angeles all offered exciting construction work. The State Capitol Building, city halls, luxurious hotels, and of course, the railway system were all on the drawing boards.

In 1875, about the time that heavy rains were again wiping out the established stage routes through the mountains, far-reaching plans were being sketched out on the top of a bar in one of San Francisco's popular saloons.

With empty shot glasses placed here and there for landmarks, and dampened fingers with which to draw, James G. Fair traced a route for a railroad system that would come from the Oakland/Alameda area, south to Newark. From there it would cross the San Francisco Bay by ferry, proceed down to San Jose, once back on dry land, and then head directly across the valley for Los Gatos, and the Santa Cruz Mountains. His finger didn't stop - the route he continued to trace traversed the mountains and would end up in Santa Cruz! Fair's on-looker, Alfred E. "Hog" Davis, took a long swig of whisky when he realized the scope and magnitude of such an undertaking.

There was no doubt about the growing need for an improved transportation system. The quicksilver mines were booming (now that quicksilver was being used for other purposes), along with the timber industry and the tanneries. There were now bearing fruit orchards along the mountain route whose ranchers needed a more efficient way to get their produce to the market place. And over in Santa Cruz, the powder works, fishing industry and expanding port facilities were all in need of a better way to overcome the problems of mountain travel.

Both men sipped their drinks in silence as they studied the sketch on their unlikely drawing board. Money was no obstacle. Fair, known as one of the Bonanza Kings, had become a millionaire when the Consolidated Virginia Mine in Nevada revealed a veritable treasure of silver deep beneath the streets of Virginia City. He also felt that the feasibility of the proposed railroad was not as far fetched as it appeared, since it was his intention to install narrow gauge. Parts for such a system were readily available through catalogues, and the tracks could easily be assembled on a three foot separation with simple hand tools.

Both Fair and Davis had survived enough prior business dealings (some considered not all that honest by their colleagues, however) to at least establish their names and reputations within the business community. Neither would have won a popularity contest, but with the idea of the railroad and the financing on their side to start with, they cared little what others thought of them personally.

A Board of Directors was hastily assembled, and on March 28, 1876, the South Pacific Coast Railroad Company was incorporated with capital stock of one million dollars. Al Davis agreed to take the presidency and young Thomas Davis, Al's nephew, was appointed Chief Engineer. It was Fair's intention to remain in the background. He was the first to recognize that the fewer times his name was mentioned in association with the venture, the better.

Young Davis immediately set off to examine the mountain situation, and reported back to the Board some serious and unfortunate miscalculations. Instead of making his own surveys, he relied on two already existing ones made by companies operating short lines up the coastal canyons out of Santa Cruz. Unfortunately, they were not all that accurate to begin with, and, in addition, only covered a portion of the easiest area to be traversed. His estimate of the number of tunnels that would be required near the summit was also erroneous, and his not accounting for the steep grades and dangerous curves between the existing surveys and reality resulted in an eventual staggering increase in construction costs.

As a matter of interest, according to author/historian Bruce MacGregor, the minuscule but already well established narrow gauge line known as the Santa Cruz and Felton, was constructed, owned and operated by much more reliable and competent people. Built by F. A. Hihn in 1874, its primary functions were to carry out lime and lumber from the canyons above Santa Cruz (a seven mile run), and passengers from Santa Cruz south along Monterey Bay to Watsonville. It was a very successful operation long before Fair and Davis hatched their trans-mountain plans on top of the oaken bar. Conceivably, with the proper financial backing, the Santa Cruz and Felton might just have beaten the South Pacific Coast with a line of its own through the mountains.

CHAPTER 25

RAILROAD CONSTRUCTION

By 1877, a labor force, made up primarily of Chinese immigrants, was blasting and clearing its way up Cat's Canyon out of Los Gatos for South Pacific Coast (S.P.C.). A freight shed, small passenger depot, engine terminal and a one-stall roundhouse had been built in Los Gatos to facilitate the moving of materials and supplies up the north face of the mountains.

The Board of Directors' decision to maintain a grade of ninety feet per mile required a continuous network of cuts and fills, tunnels and trestles. The proposed grade zigzagged eight times across the creek bed in Cats' Canyon alone, and at each point, a trestle of giant redwood timbers had to be constructed. The grading costs soared to $ 110,000 per mile, a far cry indeed from young Davis' estimate of $ 20,000. And this new figure did not begin to take into account the damage and replacement costs incurred during the heavy winter rains when disastrous washouts occurred.

Tunnel construction beneath the summit turned out to be not only costly money-wise, but extremely hazardous as well. The first tunnel to be drilled - a short bore near Alma - suffered a total cave-in, and one of the two summit tunnels, the longest at 6115 feet, from Wrights to Laurel, became the fiery graveyard for one entire workcrew and its foreman.

Chinese workman had been drilling, blasting and clearing debris from deep within the ground for several months progressing at a rate of about 10 feet per day, according to author Stephen Payne. A vein of bituminous coal had been discovered during the blasting operations, and in the days that followed, the resulting leaking gas smelled more and more strongly of petroleum. To compound the problem, oil was simultaneously discovered at Moody Gulch, not far away, at a site previously drilled in the early 1860's. When oil rose 75 to 85 feet in the hole, there were further efforts to open the strata.

At the tunnel site, a wave of uneasiness had swept through the workmen. They could not shake the Doomsday prophecy of one of the men that something awful was about to happen.

On that fateful evening, in the lead of his night shift, foreman M. C. Highland disappeared within the dark confines of the tunnel. It was his unpleasant task to flash out the small pockets of natural gas that continued to accumulate therein with alarming regularity. He used a long pole on which was tied some burning debris. Two thousand feet into the bore, as they approached the rock heading where work was to resume, Highland and the crew were apprehensive but still not expecting the total disaster ahead.

Gas seeping into the tunnel at an ever-increasing rate, had accumulated in a massive quantity. The next match Highland struck set off a deafening explosion that could be heard for miles around. A ball of fire swept back down the tunnel and shot out of the entrance, searing everything in its path. The resulting concussion outside tossed a 10-ton compressor, a horse and its wagon, and flatcars waiting on a siding into the air, around the construction yard, and down into the adjacent canyon.

A pall of silence and gloom settled over the area. There were only two survivors, (one of them, ironically, Highland himself), who clung tenaciously to life for a few more hours. but, tragically, the tunnel disaster finally claimed all of its thirty-three victims.

In the days to follow, fear ran rampant among the other Chinese crewman, and they refused to even enter the bore, much less work it. Two weeks went by, much to the consternation of the S.P.C. officials who were anxious to resume the tunnel project. A crew of hardy Welchmen, brought up from the Almaden Quicksilver Mines only lasted a matter of days before they, too, quit on the spot. It was not only the fear of another explosion that kept the superstitious miners out of the tunnel, but the fear of the "ghosts" who had seemed to take up residence there.

The other long tunnel, which was being dug simultaneously from both ends between Laurel and Glenwood, was to be 5,792 feet in length. It, too, was plagued with seeping oil and water and it suffered more than one major explosion with fatalities during its construction.

Even years later, when the railroad was in full operation and carloads of happy excursionists passed through these tunnels daily, a feeling of uneasiness would grip the passengers and crew alike. Not even the sunlight and overwhelming beauty of the countryside, once out in the open, could immediately chase it away.

Photograph of the ornate woodburner locomotive the "San Mateo" of the San Francisco and San Jose Railroad. It had the distinction of pulling the first train into San Jose in January of 1864, over 130 years ago. Photograph courtesy of William A. Wulf.

The community of Wrights, circa 1890, was reportedly the eyesore of the lot. In the words of authoress Josephine McCracken, as quoted from Stephen Payne's A HOWLING WILDERNESS, "Wrights...has a depot, hotel, store, post office, blacksmith shop, besides a number of decidedly ugly and disgraceful-looking Chinese stores and wash-houses." But neither she nor Payne understated the area's importance as a shipping center. Wrights also boasted a mountain school, fruit packing plant, railway maintenance station and the infamous "Tunnel Saloon". The entrance to Wrights Tunnel (the longest of the seven bores in the system) can be seen as a gaping, yawning black hole beyond and to the right of the water tower. Initially, a simple opening, with a wooden facer, by 1893 it boasted a massive concrete facer which had to be constructed to protect the entrance from erosion and mud slides. Photograph courtesy of William A. Wulf.

A view at Laurel, circa 1910, near the entrance to the Glenwood Tunnel, showing the tracks as they come into the station. Laurel, named for the trees (also known as Bay), found in abundance there, was situated on a ledge in a fairly steep and heavily wooded canyon, about 700 feet below the summit. "In 1880," according to author Stephen Payne, "Laurel became the most important shipping point for lumber in the Santa Cruz Mountains." One of the mills, operated by S.P.C., "produced timbers for the many tunnels and railroad ties for the road bed. Laurel was also the main storage point for firewood used to fire the steam boilers of the railroad engines." The area also serviced all of the Highland-Skyland shipping and passenger needs. Today, with the passing of the timber industry and the shutting down of the railroad, and very little through traffic, about all that is left is a quiet little community of homes. The only use of the railroad facilities remaining is that of the tunnel which has been developed as a source of water for the area. Photograph courtesy of William A. Wulf.

The Elusive "Light at the End of the Tunnel."

Looking into the Laurel Portal all the way to Glenwood indicates a truly remarkable engineering feat - a one-and-a-quarter mile, straight-as-an-arrow tunnel. The second set of tracks shown, according to William A. Wulf, was a spur line that ran from Glenwood to Laurel. Shortly after exiting the tunnel at Laurel the line dropped down the extremely steep terrain to the Hihn Lumber Mill. Because of the incline, the flat cars had to be carefully lowered with the assistance of a powerful steam winch and strong steel cables. This was always a very dangerous operation. At the mill, the lumber was loaded aboard and the cars were then winched back up the mountain side before being pulled by the waiting engine through the tunnel for delivery to Glenwood and other destinations. Photograph courtesy of William A. Wulf.

CHAPTER 26

TRACKS, TRESTLES, AND TUNNELS

The South Pacific Coast Railroad reached Los Gatos in 1878. Then, with each newly laid section of narrow gauge line, the train system penetrated deeper and deeper into the mountain range, encroaching on the stage route. Even though stage driver George Colgrove saw the end of an era coming, he continued to operate his stagecoach service. Twice he moved his base of mountain operations to connect with the train passengers, as new railroad facilities cropped up first at Lexington and then at Alma.

A temporary hotel sprang up also at Alma to accommodate the fifty or so railroad engineers, bridge builders and track layers who were stationed there. And in direct competition, the Forest House opened. Mrs. Cook, the proprietress, hoped to also capture the "tourist trade" by serving dinner to the train passengers connecting with the stage.

In 1879, Colgrove was forced to move the stage terminus one more time - to Wrights, the last stop below the summit. The stage continued to operate for one more year, during the construction of the big tunnels, but finally succumbed to progress. Colgrove's talents, however, had not gone unnoticed by the railroad officials. President of the line, Al Davis, enticed him to change his profession. After a period of training, Colgrove became 2nd conductor on the South Pacific Coast's newly acquired Santa Cruz and Felton run.

With major construction projects on both sides of the mountain, S.P.C. took advantage of the existing lines and acquired controlling interest so that they could more readily furnish their own supplies. All of the iron that was laid from the Santa Cruz side to the summit was first shipped down from San Francisco on barges and then hauled up to Felton on the trains. It was unloaded there, and then, as needed by the workcrews, hauled "up to the front."

An entry from Colgrove's diary indicates, "They kept us pretty busy. I used to have to take care of the ties and take a car load of railroad iron and rails up to the front and unload them and go back and get a load of bridge timbers, take them to the bridgeman, and run up gravel to the Chinamen to ballast the rails." Sometimes they made seven or more trips a day.

It took what seemed like a long time, but the crew finally made it up as far as Glenwood. There, forward progress came to a definite halt in a large grassy meadow. Straight ahead, 700 hundred feet below the summit, lay the Glenwood to Laurel tunnel which was still under construction. The topography of the area is such that Laurel, situated at about the same elevation as Glenwood, was to have the distinction of having two portals. The Glenwood to Laurel tunnel was being bored under one mountain ridge running roughly north to south, while the Laurel tunnel to Wrights was being bored through another ridge running along the summit of the mountains. The two portals at Laurel were separated by a distance of approximately one half mile.

The Glenwood to Laurel bore continued to be plagued with oil and water seepage problems, which made progress slow and precarious. While they waited for the underground crews to punch through the rock barrier, the other workcrews concentrated on widening, filling the cuts, and shoring up the tracks with piles. A water tank, siding and engine turntable were constructed in the meadow in anticipation of the tunnel completion.

Charley Martin had built a general store in the Glenwood area of which he was sole proprietor. He was now, 7 years later, reaping the benefits of having the railroad crews more or less stuck there. The year was 1880 and Charley's store had incorporated a United States Post Office. By spring, all the tunnel work had been completed except for the bore that had proved to be the most costly and the most deadly in the series - the one from Laurel to Wrights. Chinese crews eventually did agree to return to work there after the fatal accident, as all attempts to organize other work parties failed.

Finally, on April 11th, at about 10:00 o'clock on a Sunday morning, a final blast of black powder opened the bore, and the connection between Laurel and Wrights was made at last. The relieved and exuberant workmen poured out of the tunnel, dropping their tools along the way. They headed for the hotel where they celebrated with a round of whisky in the infamous Tunnel Saloon, a kind of a "dug-out place" in the side of the mountain. According to Stephen Payne in his book A HOWLING WILDERNESS, the owner/saloon keeper O. B. Castle was noted for his original drink called "The Discovery" which consisted of one gallon of whisky diluted with four tablespoons of water. The drink had to be consumed at one sitting to be effective.

The area around the Tunnel Saloon eventually developed into Wrights Station, a most important railroad stop. A town, although not a very attractive one, sprang up around it.

The Laurel (or southern) portal of the Wrights Tunnel with the summit about 700-feet above.

According to Josephine McCracken, "Fir-crowned mountains frowned down upon it, (Wrights), and the hideous black mouth of the great tunnel close by is always open, with the evident and determined intention of swallowing up the train - engine, cars and all..."

By the early 1890s the yield of fruit from the Santa Cruz Mountain orchards was in great demand. Wrights Station was the focal point for shipping these fruits to the canneries down below in the Santa Clara Valley. Here the buyers of fruit and produce await the arrival of the growers on their produce-laden wagons, to make their purchases. Once the negotiations were completed, the fruits and vegetables were loaded into the waiting empty train cars for immediate transport down to the canneries. The packing crates possibly came from a local mountain box mill owned and operated by Will Chamberlain and Ned Adams. Photograph courtesy of William A. Wulf.

CHAPTER 27

COMPLETION OF THE RAILROAD

President Davis, anxious to show off his newly completed railroad, issued an order to George Colgrove: "Take half the China gang from Santa Cruz, go up to the tank siding (at Glenwood), load wood on the flat cars, and run it through to Wrights."

In Colgrove's own words, "We were the first train that ever went through the tunnels!" Then he continued, "Davis and his gang (of friends) were standing around waiting. At the station, the old man stepped out to me and said, 'Well, you are late'!"

Colgrove was not happy about carrying passengers, especially railroad officials, at this early stage of the game. But Davis insisted that he and his party ride back to Santa Cruz in the coach car. Just as Colgrove predicted, the train derailed not once, but twice along the way. It took some time to finally get to Felton where the party had dinner. Then they had the return trip to look forward to - back to Wrights where a locomotive and car would be waiting to take the visiting "firemen" back to San Jose.

This time, Davis and his cronies abandoned the comfort of the coach for the thrill of the open-air flat cars. The group had the time of their lives, whooping it up while at the same time dodging hot cinders from the smoke stack.

"Well, we finally got rid of them," was Colgrove's wry comment, once they were back at Wrights. He then had to contend with a crew of track layers who had continued to celebrate throughout the day at the local hotel. By this time, they were so drunk that they had to be braced between wooden ties on the flat cars to keep them from rolling off. And in an even more foul mood were the Chinese workmen who had been abandoned at various points along the way, and had missed their lunch!

The narrow gauge railroad, a truly monumental accomplishment, was officially scheduled to open over the Santa Cruz Mountains on May 1, 1880. The sweet smell of success, however, was to be temporarily short lived. An ominous storm brewing off the coast of Northern California finally bore down on the land masses. It rained steadily for three days and three nights. Uncontrolled water, surging down the canyons, tore everything to pieces. Sections of track were left suspended in midair at the sites of the numerous washouts. Once again the work crews were called out, and the S.P.C. finally was able to open its line on May 15th, two weeks late. In honor of the occasion, a big excursion train was run down from Alameda Point with passengers from the San Francisco ferry boats.

Who could have foretold that yet another disaster was waiting to happen?... There was a new crew that day that had never made the run over the mountains. They did not know there was a steep 126-foot downgrade out of Santa Cruz on the way to Big Trees. Too late the relief brakeman realized the potentially disastrous situation. The engine was able to traverse over the newly laid tracks, expanded from the heat of the day's sun, with nothing more serious than a bad jolt. But the flat car loaded with people sitting on make-shift seats of timbers, jumped the track and spilled its load of passengers onto the ground. There were many injuries and even some fatalities, passengers crushed to death by the timbers and the flat car, itself, so the account goes. Davis was shocked that his line should suffer such a terrible accident. Colgrove, who was not on board, was steadfast in his belief, however, that it was due to just "pure, damn carelessness!"

***

Photograph of the local Glenwood area displaying advertisements for the various resorts which were accessible from the Glenwood Train Station. It appears the buggy for Villa Fontenay was patiently waiting for passengers to arrive. The Hotel de Redwoods and The Willows Resort, which was sandwiched in-between Stetson and Skyland Roads, were actually world famous. The latter, built by A. W. Beadle, boasted a huge glass-enclosed swimming pool, kept heated with cordwood, that included both a low and a high-diving board not to mention an innovative slide. The popular resort was named for the beautiful trees on the property, not native to the area. Photograph courtesy of William A. Wulf.

CHAPTER 28

RESORTS AND SPAS ALONG THE RAILROAD

The latest train disaster did not seem to keep the businessmen, excursionists and picnickers off the train, or even dampen their enthusiasm. The excursion trains would stop in Los Gatos, a still sleepy little town cradled in the fold of the foothills, and then would continue on up the mountain to Wrights, where there was a short spur line over to the heavily wooded Sunset Park. Some of the trains went beyond to Laurel where the passengers departed for the "Hotel de Redwood" by coach or wagon. Other passengers stayed on the train to Glenwood. Whether under the redwoods or festive Japanese lanterns, depending on which park they chose, lighthearted, carefree passengers would unload baskets heaped with fresh fruit, a variety of cheese, homemade bread, dill pickles, salads, roast of lamb (destined to be pit barbecued), and kegs of beer to wash it all down.

If the crowds stayed on the train for Glenwood, they eagerly anticipated the "Magnetic Springs", about three miles down the road from the station. The Springs, so named for the high iron content in the water, had been developed by an enterprising owner of the mountain spa. Large crowds of health enthusiasts flocked here around the turn of the century. Charley Martin had also opened his own resort, known as the Glenwood Hotel, and close by was The Summer Home Farm, Villa Fontenay, and the Hotel Glen Orchy.

Many times, however, those who went up the mountain in a gay, frivolous mood, came back down quite differently. The combination of the fresh air and sun's rays, and an over-indulgence in good food and warm beer caused a level of intoxication that created many a nightmare for the crews on the returning trains. Occasionally, drunken passengers would jump, fall or be pushed from the moving platforms between the cars. And many a foot or empty flask went through the window glass to allow a little more fresh air or stretching room.

In one particular noteworthy incident, the ladies aboard had to be barricaded in a separate car for their protection. But there was little the conductors could do to save the train itself. Item by item everything not permanently attached to the inside of the cars went sailing out the windows. The boisterous drunken men showed no mercy.

Late on weekends when the mournful wail of the Picnic Train whistle would fill the night air announcing its return to Newark, John Duggan, Saloon Keeper of the Duggan House alongside the tracks, knew he could be in for trouble. On many occasions he stepped out on the porch and resignedly hung a black wreath of mourning on the front door. His establishment, with its elegant, irreplaceable barroom mirror, could very well be the next victim of the unruly, inebriated crowd.

Alma Station on the Southern Pacific Railroad in 1909. Note the mileage to San Francisco is indicted to be 57.9 miles. It was originally constructed under the South Pacific Coast Railroad ownership prior to 1880. It boasted a postal and telegraph office from which cablegrams could be sent. This station along with the wooden loading platform at Lexington was inundated by the lake created when Lexington Dam was filled on August 31, 1952. Photograph courtesy of William A. Wulf.

Wrights Station on the South Pacific Coast Railway, circa 1890. During the week, this was the hub of activity for mountain orchardists shipping their fruit and other products. On weekends and holidays, this was the stop for tourists and picnickers heading for Sunset Park, and for attractions on the summit. The passengers here are dressed in finery and some of the women are carrying elegant floral sprays. Whatever the occasion, it was an important affair. Note that the possessive apostrophe appears in Wright's on the station sign. Since the property on which the community developed belonged to the Reverend James R. Wright, the apostrophe should be included to be grammatically correct. Somewhere along the literary trail, however, authors opted either to use or not to use it. Photograph courtesy of William A. Wulf.

The community of Laurel was originally called Highland. This view, circa 1885, is from near the tunnel portal to Glenwood, and only hints at the amount of lumbering activity that went on in the area. As a note of interest, much of the lumber used to reconstruct San Francisco after the 1906 earthquake came from the Hihn lumber mill situated here. The small railroad station is evident. Laurel was a jumping off point for several resorts in the area. The portal to the other tunnel leading to Wrights, was about one-half mile further up the track and there were no facilities there. Photograph courtesy William A. Wulf.

A scene, as sketched by Billie Jensen, depicting the community of Laurel, near the entrance to the tunnel leading to Glenwood. It boasted of a General Store run by the J.C. Shuford's who leased the building from owner Earl La Porte. Note the gas pumps, in which could be seen the regular (orange) and ethyl (red) fuel through the glass.

Another view of the Hotel de Redwood, built in 1859 and opened to tourists in 1864, showing the surrounding locale. This hotel had the distinction of burning down more times than a Chinese Fireworks Factory but its popularity persisted through each rebuilding by new owners. It was a popular stagecoach way station, being situated on the all-important route from the Pacific Ocean to the inland valley of Santa Clara. The ruts caused by the many wagons and coaches are plainly visible in the foreground. Photograph courtesy of Frank Adams.

Glenwood Station, circa 1890.

The many facets of Glenwood made it one of the busiest and most popular of mountain communities. It rode to fame during the stagecoach era when it was developed and maintained by two of its early pioneering families - the McKiernans and the Martins. Then the area became famous as a shipping point for lumber, produce and wine when the South Pacific Railway Company completed its facilities there, including this station, sidings, a turntable and water tank. The spas and hotels that sprung up in response to mountain popularity in the early 1900's housed millionaires, statesmen, hunters, fishermen, and those thousands of other tourists in search of rest and relaxation. When the new state highway from Los Gatos to Santa Cruz was rerouted to a ridge top a mile or so away, and the railroad system was declining, Glenwood began to fade into history. Photograph, courtesy of William A. Wulf.

Glenwood General Store and U.S. Post Office circa 1890.

The General Store, and U.S. Post Office building at Glenwood, was situated across the road from the train station. It was built owned and operated by the enterprising Charley Martin. Photograph, courtesy of William A. Wulf.

The Glenwood Hotel, circa 1909.

The gracious and popular Glenwood Hotel was built and operated by Charley Martin. Considering the times and remote location, the Glenwood Hotel was a beautifully constructed building. It was used by the Catholic Church as a retreat in more recent years, and then demolished in 1970. Photograph courtesy of William A. Wulf.

Glenwood Hotel Postcard, circa 1910.

Souvenir postcard from the Glenwood Hotel, showing a collage of scenes depicting a group of patrons (mostly women and children) being treated to a ride across a wet, wooden-planked bridge on some sort of motorized vehicle. They come into view again, as others look on from the porch, in a horse drawn wagon, and finally are seen aboard a Yosemite Wagon traversing the creek. This wagon had benches across and a fringed canvas covering, for a nice open-air ride. Photograph of postcard courtesy of William A. Wulf.

Sketch of the Hotel Glen Orchy by Billie Jensen.

The Hotel Glen Orchy was most likely a converted private home located somewhere in the Glenwood area. The original picure appeared in the Los Gatos-Saratoga Times Observer in the late 1960's.

Glenwood Magnetic Springs Stereo-pair Postcard, circa the Christmas Season, 1885.

Another popular resort, approximately 3 miles south of the community of Glenwood, was The Glenwood Magnetic Springs. There, the hot water ran orange from iron ore deposits, but tourists were sure it was "good for what ailed you." There are people on the porch of the hotel, and at least 7 more in the foreground. This stereo pair, produces a single image capable of being visualized in 3-dimensions when looked at through a stereoscope. Photograph courtesy of William A. Wulf.

CHAPTER 29

FAMILY LIFE AT THE TURN OF THE CENTURY

Just as in years past, when tribelets of Indians chose between valley living and mountain living, groups of immigrants coming to the West had to make similar decisions. Down in the Santa Clara Valley, people of French extraction tended to cluster together. Already well established in the business community were the Thees, LeFrancs and Massons but now came the Mirassous, Pelliers, Prudhommes, Navlets and Montagues. Madame Zulema Martin's husband was tragically murdered on their trans-oceanic voyage. Even though she spoke not a word of English when she stepped off the boat in San Francisco, Madame Zulema bravely and determinedly opened a boarding house for her newly arriving countrymen.

Back up near the top ridge of the Santa Cruz Mountains, Lyman Burrell, according to author Stephen Payne, sold 1,700 acres of his land holdings to immigrant, Ernst Meyer (born in Denmark, raised in Germany), in 1881. Meyer then helped establish one of the first nationalistic mountain communities in the area to be known as Austrian Gulch by selling portions of his newly acquired acreage to other Austro-German immigrants, mostly friends and relatives whom he was able to coax over from the Old Country.

Meyer planted grapes on his property, finding the top soil rich and the southern exposure of the slopes perfect for the purpose. Within a few years, with the help of his family and friends around him, he was able to establish a winery, which he called "Mare Vista" (Ocean View), that attained a "reputation of excellence," according to Payne.

In the year 1881, Edward F. Adams bought a farm in the Skyland area of the Santa Cruz Mountains for his family. He, himself, was a school textbook salesman and later a West Coast Representative for the same Chicago-based firm, and spent most of his time away from home. What he had in mind was a safe, comfortable, healthful haven for his wife and children, where he could leave them for extended periods of time without having to constantly worry about their welfare. Also, he wanted to buy something with an investment potential.

Adams bought a portion of the property owned by Professor Charles H. Allen, then-Principal of the San Jose State Normal School. The Allen family and the H. B. Nortons (Vice Principal at the same school) were his immediate neighbors. He bought two horses, old John and Sam, and a made-to-order buckboard by the Summit Blacksmith, Rasmus Neilson, which would be safe for his wife to drive. It was low to the ground with heavy, sturdy wheels to prevent any possibility of turnovers. Then the family acquired 'Lily', a Jersey cow, and a mongrel dog dubbed 'Sport', and later an English mastiff named 'Argos'.

During the times Adams was home with his family, he planted vineyards and orchards across the crest of his land, 2,100 feet above sea level. The Monterey Bay and Pacific Ocean were in view to the southwest. There was one higher mountain ridge above them, leading to the peak known as ***Loma Prieta*** (Black Mountain), to the north.

One of his children, years later, wrote in a family biography of wonderful memories of "hauling water in barrels from the neighbors after they first moved in... of watching their father lay on his stomach to check the alignment of the newly-planted trees (he would not tolerate 'anything less than perfect')... of smelling the fragrance of the redwoods and firs, and pungent odor of the bay or laurel trees... of listening to the cooing of the wild doves, watching the cottontails, possum, chipmunks and squirrels... and perhaps best of all, breathing the pure mountain air."

Besides his regular job, Adams was also active in state politics. He helped formulate the new state Constitution and supported George C. Perkins in his successful bid for the Governorship. But by 1892, 12 years after purchasing the farm, Adams was happy to get out of politics with the excuse that he had been "elected to stay at home." He also resigned his job with the American Book Company on the hopes of going into some business of his own. What unfortunately followed was the far-reaching economic panic of 1893 where it was not possible to start a new business without a good supply of capital, of which he had none. Fortunately, he did have the farm where he and his family were able to weather the storm, which "all but paralyzed the economic life of the country and so depressed prices of fruit that most growers were in financial difficulties." Prunes, the Adams' principal crop, "were bringing pitifully low return - plums, pears and grapes, most of which were shipped to the East Coast and Europe, sometimes sold for little more than the cost of freight and selling commission."

Mrs. Adams, in an attempt to do her part, put up fruit and shipped it in attractive glass containers to a San Francisco dealer in "fancy groceries." But that was not economically feasible either. The Adams' then took in borders at the farm. They were usually "friends or friends of friends" but it brought in some additional income. Everyone, mutually, seemed to enjoy the experience.

This period of hard times was a turning point in Edward Adams' life. He "entered activities and acquired interests in public affairs that set the stage for the events in his life for which he later became best known and widely respected."

Many of the Adams' family neighbors faced the same problems when it came to caring for their livestock, and planting, irrigating, growing, picking and marketing their mountain-grown products. One of the major problems was having their "principal markets several thousand miles away, and in possessing little or no knowledge about what their fruit was worth in those markets, or even what they should receive for it when it was sold to local buyers."

And so began Mr. Adams' "participation in a pioneer movement for cooperative marketing of dried fruits." He was instrumental in organizing the Santa Clara County Fruit Exchange, which led to his "interest in the cooperation among farmers that continued the remainder of his life."

The Highland Grange was formed soon after. "It really came to life as an effective community organization when Mr. Adams proposed we establish a summer school of agriculture in which instruction would be given by members of the agricultural faculty of the University of California and a professor of economics from Stanford University."

Mr. Adams found himself in charge, and "plans for the school received wide publicity and Highland Grange became about the best known grange in the state." The first few sessions were "held near the sulphur spring redwood grove on the farm, and about 40 to 50 attended. Mornings were given to lectures on purely agricultural subjects and afternoons to lectures on economics." Adams would have liked more attendees from other areas, but nevertheless, he was satisfied with the turnout.

The following year's session, in 1897, was held in the Highland Grange Hall and dealt with economics and husbandry. Regrettably this was the last session ever held due to the fact that Adams, who had taken a job with the San Francisco Chronicle, found it impossible to commute and had to move up to the city. Other people who had been most active in the Highland Grange and the affairs of the Summer School had also left the neighborhood probably due to the adverse economic conditions, and so the community effort sadly lapsed. Mr. Adams, however, never lost interest in the intent of the club.

Out of the Summer School, short lived though it was, came an important lecture on the "dreaded disease 'Phylloxera' that attacks the roots of the plant and had ravished the vineyards of France," and was now evident in the vineyards of the Santa Cruz Mountains in 1897! Unfortunately, many of the mountain vineyards were destroyed over the next few years, in spite of the early detection, because there was no treatment available.

Through the efforts of the Highland Grange, while it was active, was also the revelation that middlemen who were the agents between the producer and the end user, and who had the control of the pricing, were misusing their power for profit. In 1894, for example, they had actually dumped untold hundreds of watermelons into San Francisco Bay to rid the market of surplus for the obvious purpose of raising the market price. The exposure of arbitrarily set fees pointed out other dishonest practices and was "the beginning for the agitation for a public market, free of middlemen." In spite of Edward Adams' efforts, the farmers and growers did not fully understand the scope of the problem, and they lost their initial fights in the State Legislature for a free market.

Off the farm, Mr. Adams became a prolific writer of note on the editorial staff of the Chronicle, a champion of several important causes, founder of the Commonwealth Club of California in 1903, and its president from 1908 - 1912, as well as a teacher.

He finally found a publisher for what turned out to be one of his landmark books, THE MODERN FARMER IN HIS BUSINESS RELATIONS. "In a humorous vein the author stated this was the one book which got more compliments and fewer customers than any other book within his knowledge." Even though it did not sell widely or as predicted, the book was highly regarded in its field in spite of Adams' tongue-in-cheek humor.

His six children, all successful in their later life and respected in their chosen careers, also harbored fond memories of their father's disciplined daily schedule when they moved back to San Francisco. Meals exactly on time. A period for gardening, in the small plot next to the house, a thorough perusal of the newspaper of the day before, hours set aside for writing and a trip to the office and return home.

"Immediately on arrival home he sat down in his Morris chair and either wrote or read until dinner, which Mother was sure to have ready promptly at 6:00 P.M. Dinner was always interesting, especially when most of the family members were still at home. He wanted each of us to recount our adventures during the day. There were always matters of interest to talk about. He usually was the first to leave the dinner table, going immediately to his Morris chair in the library and to work. It was in the library that members of the family assembled for the evening and father would grind away at his writing, undisturbed by what was said or done by those about him. About 9:00 or 9:30 he stopped writing and devoted the remainder of the evening to reading. Promptly at 10:00 o'clock was bedtime."

In 1899, Josephine Clifford McCracken, mountain resident and friend of the Adams', was well known in California literary circles for her writings and poetry. When her home was destroyed by a wild fire that raced over the summit, reducing many of the buildings and homes on Loma Prieta Avenue to ashes, she began to realize just how fragile and susceptible to disaster and misuse the forested area really was.

McCracken began a campaign for conservation of the Santa Cruz Mountains and started writing an important series of articles for the Santa Cruz Sentinel Newspaper. She was not only concerned with fire, but the ever-present men with their saws as well. At this point, she enlisted the help of prominent San Jose artist Andrew P. Hill. Between the two of them they were instrumental in saving the majestic redwoods of the Santa Cruz Mountains. They established the Sempervirens Club, a Latin term meaning "forever green."

With the interest and financial backing of several Santa Clara Valley notables - Robert E. Kenna, S.J., president of Santa Clara College, Harry G. Wells, of the San Jose Mercury News staff, Superior Court Judge John E. Richards and attorney Delphin Delmas - Hill proposed a parks bill to the California Legislature and then-Governor Henry T. Gage. Through Hill's persistent efforts, a State Park was created at Big Basin, near Santa Cruz, and remains a joy to behold today.

Forerunners of the Sempervirens Club were the two pioneers mentioned earlier, Charley McKiernan and Charley Martin. Martin, for example, refused to give in to the logging boom, steadfastly protecting the graceful giants still found in profusion in the Glenwood area today. Loggers were also denied the tempting rights to the majestic "Mountain Charley Tree", by none other than McKiernan himself. Ranking among the 20 largest trees in the world, this particular redwood found in the Glenwood canyon, stands 30 ft. in diameter and rises to a breathtaking height even without its uppermost reaches, which were whipped off by cyclonic winds some years ago.

Bushel of Wheat
Bushel of Rye
All not Ready
Holler I!

By the 1880's there were at least 5 school districts in the mountains between Los Gatos and Santa Cruz: Summit, Burrell, Highland, Wrights, and Laurel. One more, Hester Creek, was established much later, in 1906. One might wonder why so many schools in such a relatively small area? The equation was quite simple. Large families seemed to be in vogue in the late 1800's. The Schultheis' for example, raised 12 children and the Adams' family 6. It was reported that the class size at the one-room school houses ranged from 25 to 30 students and, without elaborating further, the rooms were usually filled to capacity.

At the Highland School District meeting on August 30, 1878 all the Board was present. Anson Miller was elected Chairman, and E. Spalsbury, District Clerk. Minutes of the meeting reveal:

"Ordered that the building offered by E. Spalsbury be accepted as a school house and that the clerk buy the necessary furniture at Santa Cruz.

"Ordered that George Miller be employed to haul the furniture from Santa Cruz and that a 1/2 cord stove wood be furnished by Milton Miller.

"Ordered that school be opened September 9 approximately for a term of 3 months and that Mrs. S. H. Spalsbury be employed as teacher at $ 60.00 per month. And the board adjourned."

(s) E. Spalsbury District Clerk

Minutes of the next meeting on November 27, 1878 read:
"The Board met at residence of Anson S. Miller.

The following accounts were audited:

Milton H. Miller - for wood .... $ 2.00

George Miller - for hauling .... $ 3.50

E. Spalsbury, District Clerk -
for furniture and supplies $ 16.20
And the Board adjourned."

Over the next few years, there were some interesting entries in the minutes, changes in the Board and new teachers hired. On June 6, 1885, the Board ordered:

"That posts be set in the school grounds for hitching horses.

That all hanging and dangerous branches be cut into fuel.

That pipe be bought to improve the water supply.

That no prayer meetings be held in the school-house, except

it be taken in charge by some responsible adult person."

On August 21st, 1885:

"The Board heard a complaint of Mrs. Bliss, teacher, against Delford Clough. It was unanimously voted to suspend him from school till such time as he should apologize to the teacher and promise to behave better in the future. The clerk was instructed to inform Mr. and Mrs. Clough of this and to demand that the door of a water-closet at the school which Delford had injured, be repaired at their expense. It was further ordered that the scholars should not be allowed the use of slingshots on the school grounds, and that any child guilty of throwing stones at passers-by should first be reprimanded and then, after a second offense of the same kind, be expelled."

At the December 2nd Board meeting:

"It was decided among other things, that a board partition should be erected on the school grounds between the boys' and the girls' water-closets. And Mr. Slaughter was appointed to attend to this business."

On February the 10th, 1886:

"Trustees all met at the house of Mrs. Milton Miller. It was decided that School should be opened on the 8th of March next, unless a severe storm at that time should be present; in which case, the time should be postponed a week or two longer."

On June 10th, 1887:

"The trustees then listened to a complaint from Mrs. Clough relative to her boy having been kept after school against her expressed wishes, and made to sweep the school house. Mr. Slaughter stated that Mrs. McCracken (teacher), in doing this, was acting under his instructions. It was the opinion of the remaining two members of the Board, that Mr. Slaughter had exceeded his powers, and that the trustees have no right to enforce rules in school requiring manual labor of children against the parents' wishes. Quite a spirited discussion followed and then the meeting adjourned."

Bushel of Wheat
Bushel of Clover
All not Hid
Can't Hide Over

Young girls assignment in Home Economics, circa 1890. Miriam Skipp, student, details her Underwear Budget for the year.

Celebration at Burrell School

July 4, 1890

To Celebrate the Raising of the First Flag

Bought with Proceeds of an Entertainment Prepared by

"The Ten" Past and Present Pupils Drilled by:

Mrs. M.B. Smith in Readings and Recitations

PROGRAM

Opening Program	Rev. J. R. Wright
Dedication	Ben Ferris
Oration	Will Sears
Solos	Miss Daisy Karr
Closing Prayer and Benediction	Rev. A. E. Sears
Raising of the Flag	Miss Minnie Morrell

A photograph will be taken after the exercises.

In 1887, John Schultheis and his neighbors constructed the Summit Opera House. It was a frame structure 45 feet wide by 75 feet long. Everyone for miles around felt a rush of excitement upon its completion, for now there would be ample room for weddings, church socials, box-luncheons and dances.

"Nothing would stop the mountain people from coming to a dance!" as Stephen Payne put it in his book A HOWLING WILDERNESS. "It seemed to be the most popular social event of the late 1880's and early 1900's."

There were several local musicians whom Schultheis, a musician himself, recruited into a community orchestra. They had a grand piano, accordion, guitar, banjo, and several violins. Traveling road companies of actors and other entertainers were also booked into the popular Summit Opera House. Even Shakespearean plays were well attended by the local citizenry. According to Payne, the Summit Social Club also used the facilities once a month and attendees came from Wrights, Skyland, Laurel, Glenwood, Los Gatos and Burrell.

The settlers of the Santa Cruz Mountains brought so many varied religious beliefs with them, that it took some time to organize a church. Up until the late 1870's the father-figure of each household probably read from the scriptures, and brief prayers were said before meals and bedtime. When compatibility between neighbors finally revealed similarities in beliefs, people opened their homes for Sunday meetings. School houses also did double duty serving as chapels on the Sabbath for Sunday School meetings and regular services.

Finally, two churches were built, according to Payne, the Skyland Presbyterian Church, in 1887, and Wrights Presbyterian Church, in 1893. Both were founded by Reverend Mitchel. Many local residents contributed their time and materials to the construction of these two buildings. Payne relates an amusing story of pickets donated by W. A. Young (reluctantly, for he was not an avid church-goer) for a fence around Skyland Church. When the fence never went up and the donated fencing material was nowhere in sight, the donor peeked inside the building one day. There were his pickets in a wood box by the stove to be used for fuel! "He never went inside the place again!"... But the final line had not been written yet. The Reverend Mitchel ran off with a married woman, so the story goes. The distraught husband disappeared, as well, after his house burned in a suspicious fire. No bones were found in the ashes and so the mystery persists to this day. - Amen.

Listed below are some of the names of the families who initially settled in the Highland and Skyland Ridge area, as well as the names of other key figures who worked or lived in the Summit, Lexington, Glenwood and Laurel areas from the 1850's up to the turn of the century:

The "Good Guys"...

Adams	*Fidel*	*Meyer*
Allen	*Goldman*	*Miller*
Bassett	*Gould*	*Montgomery*
Bean	*Gray*	*Morrell*
Burrell	*Hadsell*	*Norton*
Chamberlain	*Harlow*	*Rankin*
Clough	*Hanks*	*Rapp*
Coldren	*Jones*	*Rogers*
Colgrove	*Knox*	*Schultheis*
Cox	*Martin*	*Sears*
Crane	*Maynard*	*Slaughter*
Dickerson	*McCracken*	*Spalsbury*
Dodge	*McKiernan*	*Stetson*
Emery	*McEwen*	*Thompson*
Feely	*McMurtry*	*Wright*
		Young

The "Bad Guys"...

Garcia	*Hamilton*	*Murrietta*
Smythe	*Sydneyites*	*Vasquez*

Edward F. Adams

Delia Roxana Cooper Adams

Members of the Adams family gathered on the porch of their ranch at Skyland, Santa Cruz Mountains, 1904. One son is missing from the group picture. Photograph courtesy of Frank Adams.

At the turn of the century, members of the Edward Adams family at a typical evening get-together. The usual after-dinner sessions included reading, writing, piano playing, exchanging of ideas, and recounting the day's adventures. Even the family dog takes part. Photograph courtesy of Frank Adams.

The Adams' Skyland ranch house, and upper portion of their orchard, circa 1890. Photograph courtesy of Frank Adams.

Photograph, taken in December 1893, of the Adams' Grove, a secluded retreat on the Skyland Ranch used by the family and also the Highland Grange Summer School. The missing trees shown as stumps, were felled by W.A. Young, Sr. in 1871 and 1872. They were hauled to the Chase's Lumber Mill (now Halls Bridge). Photograph courtesy of Frank Adams.

A view of Colonel Slaughter's Lagoon, which was fed by artesian wells, in 1893. Years later, after going dry, the area became the site of Adolph Rapp, Jr.'s pear orchard. Photograph courtesy of Frank Adams.

Colonel Slaughter in front of his home near the summit of the Santa Cruz Mountains. Photograph courtesy of Frank Adams.

Sunday Outing with Baby. Photograph courtesy of Frank Adams.

According to Emma Mae (Rapp) Lydon, her maternal grandfather, Hiram Ingraham, was delivered into this world by an Indian woman in a small Indian village off the dirt trail while his mother and father were en route from Connecticut to the West Coast in the mid 1800s. In spite of many tragedies and hardships, specifically the death of his parents and the breakup of his siblings when he and the others were put up for adoption, Hiram matured into a self-reliant, self-educated man of great physical stamina and moral character. He became a leader among the early settlers of the Santa Cruz Mountains. He married, and his wife, Susan (Smith), he found to be a warm and compassionate woman who devoted her life to helping others. She read a book on how to bring babies into this world and was responsible for delivering many of the offspring of the original pioneers. When her own daughter, Emma Bessie, went into labor, Susan was hurriedly fetched by horse and buggy to orchestrate as midwife. Finally, the men in the area decided that being isolated, as they were, was not good in case of dire medical emergencies. Under the direction of Hiram, they strung telephone lines along the mountain roads and through their orchards of plum and cherry trees, so that residents could "hook on," establishing the Mountain Telephone Company, later purchased by Bell. The minuscule phone company building was located across from Burrell School and next door to one of Hiram's two mountain stores. These were popular places where one could find everything from "needles and threads to chicken feed," Emma Mae continued. One time, a little boy was nosing around in her grandfather's Skyland Store, peeking under every bushel and basket he could reach. When asked what in the world he was looking for he replied, "I want to see where Grandma Ingraham keeps her babies!" Hiram and Susan's daughter, Emma Bessie, became the mountain area's first U.S. Postmistress. Descendants of this hardy pioneer family still live in the area today, along with descendants of other families, the Fidel, Sears, Taylor, Mancarti and Adams.

Looking northwest from the porch of the Crane (and later the Rapp) Ranch, in 1893. The orchard shown is relatively young. Photograph courtesy of Frank Adams.

A panoramic view in 1893 showing three ranches - the Allen's (left), the Norton's (center), and the Reverend Float's cabin (right). Today, both the Norton house and Float cabin are gone. Photograph courtesy of Frank Adams.

Father / Daughter
Will Chamberlain and daughter, Alice, January 1877. Chamberlain was a friend and college class-mate of Ned Adams, one of Edward Adams' sons. The two of them became partners in a box mill supplying shipping crates to the fruit growers. Much of the lumber they used came from the Adams' Ranch. Photograph courtesy of Frank Adams.

Unidentified, but possibly Lavinia Cooper, the mother of Delia who married Edward Adams. The elaborate dress is Civil War era. Photograph courtesy of Frank Adams.

At least six ladies in front of a Santa Cruz Mountains farm house. The young man on the wagon is apparently waiting for his passengers to board. Could the lady (third from right) possibly be in mourning? She is dressed in black complete with veil. Note the elaborate windmill which ran the water pumping system. Also note the picket fencing which was abundant in the area, and locally available from the box mills. The blank area on the photograph is due to a damaged section of the print. Photograph courtesy of Frank Adams.

Violins at the Saw Mill.

A one-horse-powered saw mill in the 1890's, perhaps belonging to William A. Young who owned and operated such a box and shingle mill in the Highland-Skyland area. Note that the horse is being serenaded to lighten his work load. Photograph courtesy of Frank Adams.

On the veranda, in the mid 1890's, are Miss Wakeley, Miss Sargent, and her mother, and Mr. Sargent with his prized pipe and faithful dog, 'Captain'. Photograph courtesy of Frank Adams.

Unknown gentlemen having a peaceful smoke in the library. Note the family photographs and collectibles that surround him. Also the pipe is very similar to the one that was being smoked by Mr. Sargent. Photograph courtesy of Frank Adams.

Highland School Class, circa 1893.

An 1893 picture, of the Highland School class. Katherine Adams, one of the daughters of Edward Adams, is the teacher on the right, rear; Mrs. Laurea Miller, teacher, is shown at left, rear. Note the high-top shoes, croquet mallets, kick ball and air pump. Photograph courtesy of Frank Adams.

First Flag Raising at Burrell School on July 4, 1890.

This event was in honor of the rebuilding of the School by local residents after the first School burned to the ground. There were over 100 interested people in attendance. The participants are seated on the make-shift stage along with a pump organ. Note the young rifleman in the front row of the audience. The program for the event appears elsewhere in the text (p. 103). Photograph courtesy of Frank Adams.

The Laurel School as sketched by Billie Jensen.
The twin-tower design made this little schoolhouse unique in the mountain districts. It was still standing, although in a state of disrepair, in the 1970's.

Class picture at one of the larger schools in the mountain area, circa 1890. Note the rather formal attire and emphasis on hats and bows. Photograph courtesy of Frank Adams.

Croquet at Highland School in 1893

The purpose of this popular game was to, in turn, successfully hit your wooden ball with your wooden mallet through metal wickets laid out in a course. Whoever got to the finish post without missing a wicket or breaking any of the other rules, won the game! Photograph courtesy of Frank Adams.

The Skyland Church, built in 1887, is still a house of worship today. This photograph was taken not long after completion. The founding pastor was Reverend Mitchel, a controversial character. Photograph courtesy of Frank Adams.

An 1890 photograph of preparations to create a "Wedding Chapel" somewhere in the summit area. Since the room is quite large perhaps the site is the Summit Opera House, or one of the mountain hotels. Note that the arbor and doves are anchored to a good-sized chandelier. Photograph courtesy of Frank Adams.

A late 1800's photograph taken of three local residents during an outing. Fishin' or Huntin' - that is the question. Maybe they haven't asked the dog yet. Note the man is wearing the lady's hat and vice versa, hinting that they were out to have a good time. Photograph courtesy of Frank Adams.

A photograph taken of a friendly poker game being played outside under the arbor, circa 1890. A child watches from the doorway as two of the men seem to be splitting the pot but there is more wine in the bucket, and the winds of fortune could change. Some of the faces are familiar but not identified. Photograph courtesy of Frank Adams.

Unidentified ranch house, circa 1890, somewhere near the summit. Landscaping was in progress and a white picket fence would soon surround the home. Photograph courtesy of Frank Adams.

These Santa Cruz Mountain children were fortunate, they were treated by their father to a day they no doubt remembered all the rest of their lives - the Opening Day of the PPIE (Panama-Pacific International Exposition). On the shores of San Francisco Bay, a complete "Emerald City", right out of the Land of Oz, was built to commemorate the opening of the Panama Canal in 1915. Amazing special effects, elegant buildings and statuary, thousands of illuminating pastel lights, bejeweled tower, exhibits and new inventions to stagger the mind, International and State pavilions, food and Fun Zone combined to make this the Exposition of all times. Willard E. Worden, was the Exposition's Official Photographer, capturing the magic just as he did the devastation of the 1906 Earthquake. Photograph courtesy of Frank Adams.

This picture, from the Adams' collection, may have been taken because of an interesting, perhaps amusing, coincidence in names. When Mr. Adams was in San Francisco on his many bookselling business trips, he enjoyed staying at the rather elegant Cosmopolitan Hotel on Market Street. The hotel photographed here, by the same name, appears to be more of the mountain lodge genre, with patrons ready to go hunting or fishing. Note the gentleman with the rifle and dog, and the lady with the long pole and wicker creel. Photograph courtesy of Frank Adams.

The Ol' Swimmin' Hole.

No self respecting mountain area, teeming with children, would be complete without one! Photograph courtesy of Frank Adams.

General area around either the Summit or Highland Road. Note the log house under construction in the lower right. Photograph courtesy of Frank Adams.

The Santa Cruz Mountains with a view of the Crane Orchard (later the Rapp Ranch) circa 1893. Other developments (cleared land areas) can be seen in the background. Photograph courtesy of Frank Adams.

In the early 1940's, Highland School, in the Summit area of the Santa Cruz mountains, designed a KITCHEN of the FUTURE which was on display at either the Pre-World War II Santa Clara County Fair, or the Santa Cruz County Fair. Both were held in tents at this time. Of special interest was a newfangled appliance called a "Pressure Cooker." This was a utensil developed around 1940, for cooking or preserving foods by means of superheated steam under pressure - effective but dangerous. If defective or not used properly, the pot with its escaping steam could scald the cook or send the whole kitchen right into the future! Photograph courtesy of Frank Adams.

Since the community of Highland-Skyland was a bustling farm and orchard center, the Open-Air Market evolved. There were no written references to this facility in other books researched and so it might lead one to believe that it was short-lived. Photograph courtesy of Frank Adams.

A horse named "Mike" with rider who looks very much like one of the girls on Page 129. Photograph courtesy of Frank Adams.

There are more children in this photograph than meet the eye at first glance. From Mid-Winter Scenes in the Santa Cruz Mountains courtesy of Frank Adams.

CHAPTER 30

1893 - A WILD AND WOOLLY WINTER

"The Los Gatos Mail", Los Gatos, California, January 19, 1893:

"The recent great storms have played havoc with the railroad near Wrights, causing a serious caving in of the tunnel - the principal break occurring about 100 feet from the mouth of the tunnel, nearest Wrights - extending back nearly 300 feet, and all efforts to stop the sliding mass of earth and rocks have thus far proved futile. Timbers measuring one foot in diameter placed to check the in-rolling mass were crushed like pipe stems and no other course was left but to cut away the portion of the mountain directly over the tunnel, and for nearly 3 weeks this work has been going on, with a force of nearly three hundred men, plying their axes, crow-bars, picks and shovels, and it seems quite probable that it will require fully one month more to complete the work and insure the safety of the tunnel in the future.

"This damaged tunnel is over one and a half miles in length, and there is no way to transfer freight and passengers over the narrow gauge, and as a natural consequence, all travel between these points go over the broad gauge by way of Watsonville. As a result of the cave-in, the through trains have been abandoned, running from Alameda to Wrights and return. The local trains from Santa Cruz, north to Glenwood and Boulder Creek, run as usual, as also does the Los Gatos train.

"It is a good thing that as it did happen, it happened at this time of the year, before the regular spring travel sets in over this road which is so popular to the traveler and tourist who enjoy its scenic beauty."

* * *

This incident necessitated the total revamping of the tunnel entrance at Wrights. The simple wooden facer had been completely destroyed in the mudslide brought on by the unrelenting rains. It was replaced later in the spring, when things dried out, with a massive concrete portal.

* * *

From the Life Story of George L. Colgrove:

On May 7, 1895, a large party of railroad conductors was to travel East for the Grand Division Meet in Atlanta, Georgia. There weren't quite enough railroad people available to warrant the special excursion train, so a party of eighty was finally mustered by inviting some outsiders.

A Southern Pacific Engine was chosen to pull the chartered train made up of three Pullmans, a baggage car, and a dining car. At the last minute, when asked for donations of provisions, San Jose and other area merchants eagerly responded for the publicity. "There was a man by the name of Swinford who had a winery in the Santa Cruz Mountains and he donated two jugs full of his wine. Mr. Malpass from Los Gatos sent a case of champagne." Southern Pacific pulled the conductors' special as far as Ogden, Utah, where Union Pacific took over and pulled them the rest of the way to Atlanta for the 3-day convention.

Then the California contingency turned up the Eastern Seaboard, making many stops and taking several interesting side trips, including a lay-over in Baltimore where they all managed to get sick on oysters. Then they headed up into Canada before the train turned West. They reported a fabulous stop in Chicago at the Tremont House, and also in Banff, where Colgrove revealed they feasted on cold turkey and champagne, poached salmon, fresh strawberries and creamy custard pie.

* * *

CHAPTER 31

HAIR RAISING RIDES ON THE NARROW GAUGE

Near the turn of the century, a series of accidents began to plague the railroad almost on a regular basis. Although one of the first did not take place in the Santa Cruz Mountains, nor was it on narrow gauge, it was one of the most serious and shocking.

On Decoration Day (May 30th) in 1890, the Southern Pacific broad gauge 1:15 local was crossing the estuary near Oakland. It was packed with crowds of people planning to attend memorial graveside services at Oakland cemeteries. Equipment failure and inattentiveness of the crew to note that a swing bridge over one of the many creeks was in use to allow the passage of a yacht, were the causes of the disaster. Brakes jammed on at the last minute failed to slow the locomotive's progress. It careened off the end of the tracks into the murky water fifteen feet below. Then the first car tilted crazily sideways, up-ended, and plunged into the water on top of it. Thirteen people drowned. In mute testimony, freshly cut flowers, originally destined for other graves, floated to the surface.

Two years later, again on Decoration Day, a "Flatcar Special" on the narrow gauge was traversing the abrupt curves in Cat's Canyon, above Los Gatos. Suddenly, the cars came uncoupled. Happy picnic-bound passengers, heading for Sunset Park, were flung helter-skelter off the flat cars. Although there were no fatalities this time, the sharp rocks and hard scrabble along the tracks was not the best nor softest landing site! The shocked, furious and injured passengers took out against the hapless crew, and might have lynched an engineer or two had there been any rope handy.

On the eve of Thanksgiving, 1893, dispatchers from both Los Gatos and Santa Cruz sent engines up to the Laurel Tunnel. The Los Gatos switcher heading south, had an assignment at the Laurel end of the tunnel, and the Santa Cruz engine, heading north, was to move some freight at the Wrights end of the tunnel. Deep within the bore, probably not too far from the site of the blast that took the lives of so many construction workers a few years before, the two engines, following their conflicting orders, met head-on.

Once again, surprisingly enough, there were no fatalities but the crewmen had to fight the darkness and the toxic fumes belching from the engines while they stumbled out the tunnel portal at Wrights, a good half mile away.

Accidents and derailments also stalked the logging trains operating out of the Boulder Creek and Felton areas. The weight of the heavily laden flat cars was many times too much for the light, narrow gauge rails. The trains' speed and pitch, combined with the sharp curves and steep grades, whipped the tracks, loosened the connecting pins and separated the joints. The lucky engineers "rode the ties" when their trains jumped the tracks; the unlucky ones many times lost their lives in tragic, grinding crashes.

Engineer Stanley, injured in one accident was later killed in another at Big Trees, near Tunnel # 6. The engine jumped the tracks and ran against the bank, crushing him. Fireman Henry Coil was badly injured in the same tragic mishap.

Understandably, the public began to feel apprehensive about the safety of narrow gauge transportation. The accidents and inevitable lawsuits were beginning to take their toll on the enterprise that had accomplished so much. For a brief period in time, some of the previously inaccessible areas and mysteries of the Santa Cruz Mountains had been unlocked.

The broad gauge railroad was coming into its own. In 1887 South Pacific Coast Railroad leased its system to Southern Pacific Railroad. On a special train tour of the narrow gauge Leland Stanford, founder of Stanford University in 1885, wrote a check to James Fair for a total of two million dollars for the 55-year lease. It was Stanford's intent to change the system, now renamed South Pacific Coast Railway to standard gauge. By 1895 the new standard gauge third rail had been laid from Santa Clara to Los Gatos. Then, once again, the engineers stood at the base of the mountains...those "almost impossible mountains"... shaking their heads at the obstacles they knew lay just beyond the first curve of the track. There was no choice, however. The trend was definitely away from narrow gauge and the railroad officials were actually anxious to make the switch-over.

During the next six years, work never ceased on revamping the entire line over the mountains. Before the third rail could be installed, increasing the distance between rails to four feet eight and one-half inches which was necessary to accommodate the standard size trains, there was much widening and shoring up of the track bed to be done. The tunnel system, like 'deja vu', proved to be the most staggering and costly of engineering feats.

The first short bore in Los Gatos Creek near Alma had to be blasted open, once and for all, and this was accomplished in 1903. It had long plagued the railroad system with its rock slides and proximity to the water flume which clung to the mountain side only a few feet above the top of the tunnel. The second tunnel, at Wrights, collapsed during the widening operation, proving to many that ghosts still did abide there.

By 1903, the third rail had reached Wrights, and by 1905 the work of conversion was almost complete. There was one short 10-mile stretch left to be done, from Wrights over the summit to Felton. The worst and the "longest" 10 miles had been left for last.

According to a news article in the Los Gatos Mail, which appeared Thursday, April 5, 1906, "It may be a year or several years before that part of the work is done but for the present, narrow gauge service will be cut down at least one-half, and perhaps two-thirds or three-quarters, all depending on where the transfer point will be established. Los Gatos is making the effort to have that business here. It may be at Santa Clara, San Jose, Campbell, Los Gatos or Wrights..."

CHAPTER 32

LOS GATOS' CHINA CAMP

During the peak of railway construction, repair and conversion to broad gauge, a China Camp was established along the banks of Los Gatos Creek. It was primarily made up of tents, rickety shacks and bedrolls but, according to the late Father William Abeloe, historian and lecturer, the community boasted close to 2,000 inhabitants (men, women and children) at one point in time.

In their traditional "Coolie Hats", the work crews posed for many photographs in front of their back-breaking accomplishments. The giant trestles and tunnel portals of the railroad system through the Santa Cruz Mountains proved a perfect backdrop.

Other Chinese became merchants and carried their goods on long slender poles across their shoulders. Their merchandise was displayed in bamboo baskets which were hung from the ends of the poles. In this fashion, they peddled their meats, fish, vegetables and cooking ware from "door to door."

The more educated the Chinese were, the better the jobs they landed. Many, as they did for Edward Adams, worked and lived on the mountain farms and ranches helping with planting, harvest, and property maintenance. Others became cooks for the lumber mills, harvest crews, railroad gangs, and some took over the kitchens in private homes. They had a penchant for succulent pork, and secret ways of preparing it along with rice dishes, that suddenly put their talents in demand.

The Lyndon family of Los Gatos established a popular Chinese laundry works on Front Street, later renamed Montebello Way. There was plenty of laundry to do, and "Sing Lee's Laundry", as it was called, survived many years at the original site.

As pointed out previously, however, prejudice and outright hatred continued to exist between many whites and Chinese. Not only that, if warring Tongs amongst the Chinese themselves were thrown together in the same community, the ethnic group suffered at its own hands. But it was the unwanted offspring of the Chinese prostitutes, that brought immediate attention to a scandalous problem, and a clash in cultural mores. Most of the female babies were immediately put to death - a long-practiced Chinese custom which Occidentals found abhorrent.

A wealthy benefactor from San Francisco, Donaldina Cameron, concerned with the alarming number of Chinese orphans at risk, established the Ming Quong Home and took them in. The home, now a school, still exists in Los Gatos, but since the need to care for Chinese orphans is no longer relevant, the purpose of the school today has changed. It still, however, is dedicated to helping and serving children with special needs.

As quickly as China Camp came into being, it began to fade away as the work crews dispersed or moved on to other sites. One day, China Camp, Los Gatos, was a bustling community, the next it was a ghost town within a town.

CHAPTER 33

LOS GATOS - "GEM OF THE FOOTHILLS"

Los Gatos was incorporated in 1887. It was often referred to as a "sleepy little town" prior to that. There were, however, reports of "53 murders in the vicinity before Garcia was hung from the Main Street Bridge in 1883." The particular Garcia mentioned here became legendary when he reportedly stabbed and killed a local man during a drunken brawl. The angry mob then spilled out of the Los Gatos hotel saloon, and chased the murderer out behind the Tollhouse where he was caught and turned over to the Sheriff.

The small, inadequate jail facility in Los Gatos was no match for the men who wanted, this time, to get in! When the excitement and initial furor died down, and most people had finally gone home, so the story goes, a small group of local townsmen pried open the jail cell door. Garcia was supposedly then marched to the Main Street Bridge - the one constructed of beautiful milled timbers - where, without further ceremony, he was lynched from one of the posts.

Another mystery! What really did happen, if anything, that night on the Main Street Bridge? Unfortunately, the source of this story remains obscure as the tale has been told and retold many times. Historian William Wulf has searched for reliable coverage of such an event through Los Gatos, San Jose, and even Santa Cruz newspapers and has found nothing. It is his feeling that the community was far too civilized by this point in time - with churches and schools, with farming and tourism, and new businesses springing up - for such a series of Wild West antics. He points out there was also a Constable, not a Sheriff, appointed to the Redwood District which included Los Gatos. Also, all law breakers, after being apprehended were to be taken to the Santa Clara County Jail, built in 1871 behind the Court House on North First Street in San Jose. But because it has not been proven one way or another that the crime actually took place, the story will remain here in this text as an unsolved mystery.

Following the supposed demise of Garcia, there came the definite demise of the lumber industry which had initially pumped life-blood into the community. (At the peak of the timber activity, there was a load of lumber either coming into or going out of Los Gatos every 15 minutes, twenty four hours a day!) When the Lexington lumber mills moved over the ridge toward Boulder Creek to more lucrative sites, Los Gatos was no longer the hub of the lumber transportation/distribution system.

The late Dora Rankin, noted local historian who wrote her memoirs for the newspaper, recalled the turn of the century years, before the influx of people:

"There were no streets nor houses - only vineyards, orchards and hayfields. The area from Massol Avenue to Santa Cruz Avenue was known as the 'Almond Grove', and in the spring, was a sea of pink and white blossoms... There were tall pines intermingled with orchards of delicious apricots and cherries... East Los Gatos was the oldest part of town, but boasted of nothing more than a string of wooden buildings, dirt streets and wooden sidewalks... About the only sounds one heard were the whistling of the trains, the ringing of the bells, and the rumble of the farm wagons as they came down from the mountains with their loads of apples, prunes and chickens... At that time, we had seven through-trains a day going to and from Santa Cruz. One could tell the time of day by the sound of the whistle or the ringing of the bell. Each train had its own particular sound... The creek which ran nearby used to overflow so often the ground was swampy and full of croaking frogs. The creek was a joy to everyone. Not only was it beautiful to look at, but was a wonderful place for recreation. Large rocks protruded into the stream, and here on top of their flat surfaces, we would have our picnics of roasted ears of corn... Further up the creek was a large pool where many of the town's boys learned to swim. Large oak and sycamore trees hung their branches over the water, giving plenty of shade on a hot summer day.

"Before the turn of the century we all lived very primitively compared to the way we live now. No electrical refrigeration or washing machines. We had a wooden icebox that opened at the top where a big chunk of ice was kept. Underneath was a pan that had to be emptied regularly or the back porch would be flooded. We also had a large, square wooden washing machine with a handle that had to be turned by hand. A wringer was attached to the side of the machine.

"The grocery boy came once a week for your order which was delivered the same day. A butcher, fish, milk, vegetable and bakery wagon had their special days for bringing around their products."

Mrs. Rankin remembered a deserted cemetery at the corner of Santa Cruz and Saratoga Avenues:

"It was truly a spooky place, all overgrown with shrubbery and a mass of oak trees. The lights and shadows played weird tricks, flashing in and out over the grey and white tombstones. And at the very corner was a little grave with

the inscription, 'Willie has gone to God'. I have wondered, all these years, just who was little Willie?"

On a lighter note, Mrs. Rankin recalled:

"Property at the corner of College Avenue and East Main Street was purchased by a group of investors from San Francisco. They built a lovely big house with a beautifully landscaped garden - the first one in town." (She did not remember the exact year but she did recall going through the house before it was completed.) "I noted the spacious rooms downstairs," she continued, *"and the very small ones upstairs. When the city fathers found out it was built for a house of ill fame, they couldn't allow such a thing. It had to be sold for a residence... after first remodeling the upstairs!"*

During the summer months, according to Mrs. Rankin, Los Gatos was full of tourists and vacationers. Every Saturday, big excursion trains came down from San Francisco and Oakland. To entertain those passengers who disembarked in Los Gatos, there were marching bands and gala parades which always wound up at the town park.

* * *

Emma Stolte was the daughter of a mountain pioneer and, in later years, another Los Gatos authoress. In a newspaper article written in the 1960's entitled " One Life, Mine", she tells a story from a different perspective - looking south up Cat's Canyon before the turn of the century.

The Stolte's lived eight miles from Los Gatos, on what is today Skyline Boulevard at the crest of the Santa Cruz Mountains. Emma tells of horse-drawn wagon days where it took two and one-half hours or so to go up the mountain from Los Gatos, depending upon the load, and the amount or dust or mud on the road, and only about one hour and fifteen minutes to come down the hill. One time she was on a runaway wagon, driven by her mother, when neighbor's dogs nipped at their horses' heels.

"Away the horses went and were soon out of control. As they turned a very sharp corner, the wagon upset and we were thrown out, and the horses clattered off up the road. Mr. Newell and his son John, who owned the dogs, came to our rescue. John picked me out of a Hazel Bush, set me up on a bank, told me not to cry as I wasn't hurt, and hurried off to catch the horses with which he soon returned. They righted the wagon, fixed what was broken, helped retrieve the scattered groceries, and we were able to go on home, somewhat shaken, but otherwise unhurt."

Emma and her little sister, Lottie, played a game whereby the trip home seemed shorter - they anticipated and called out the nick-names that had been given certain areas of the route. About a mile out of town there was a steep and narrow road that led off to the right to the Butler residence out of sight around a corner. It was closed by a gate on which a sign read "For Sale, Honey, 80 cents a gallon." Mr. Butler was known to all as "Honey Butler." (He also manufactured a tonic from local herbs which was called "Butler's Linger Longer" and was on sale in local Los Gatos stores.)

Honey Butler's was on The Grade, the three steep miles from Los Gatos to Lexington, deep with dust in the summer time and equally deep with mud in the winter.

> *"The grade was narrow with only a few wide spots where one could wait to let any rig coming the other way pass. Then, the first mile of Black Road up the mountain was known as The Dobie (possibly short for Adobe). It was without shade, unbearably hot in the summer, and very cold and muddy in winter. Then came The Brush, more sheltered from the elements and on better ground. Next was Raymond's Cut and The Water Trough, Gist's Road, and then by Newell's to Begg's Hill, The Gooseberry Patch or Spanish Flats, and the 'S' Bend, The Madrones, Stolte's Hill and finally home!"*

Emma went on to say that the road along the summit (now Skyline Boulevard) passed from one man's land to another's. There were gates (and extra gates if there were cultivated or yard areas in between) along the five or six miles with which she was familiar.

> *"From Herring's to Sharp's there was a total of fourteen gates, in spite of the fact it was a public road. Anyone could travel it who wished to. The only requirement: Shut the Gate!"*

It was up to the local residents to maintain the road from Los Gatos to the Summit:

> *"The men would gather at Lexington with their teams and tools and work their way up. It was a matter of much criticism that each man and his equipment dropped out on reaching his furthermost property line. So the last, most difficult miles were left for the few living on the summit..."*

"After some years, these roads were taken over or deeded to the Counties, Santa Clara and Santa Cruz, improvements made and their care paid for by tax money...On the Black Road, as far up as water was available, the County of Santa Clara had men with tank wagons wet down the road several times a week to keep the dust under control...

"The road along the top (Skyline) was never watered so the dust was always inches deep. People wore dusters (full length coats with high collars), and the ladies wrapped veils or scarfs over their hats and made the best of it."

Emma concluded her story with the fact that once Santa Cruz County was in control of its section, all along Skyline the gates came down! As far as she was concerned that was the greatest improvement of all.

This picture shows the northbound train, about even with Windy Point, beginning its rather steep and winding downhill grade through Cat's Canyon on its way to Los Gatos Station. The Water Flume is visible on the opposite side of the Canyon. The train's first crossing of Cat's Canyon by means of a trestle can be seen in this photograph.

This photograph shows the northbound train proceeding down the narrow gorge above Los Gatos toward the train station. The narrow gauge railroad tracks can be seen running parallel to and approximately 30-50 feet above Los Gatos Creek. The Water Flume is clearly visible on the opposite side of the canyon. The road to Santa Cruz is barely visible above the tracks. Photograph courtesy of William A. Wulf.

Do you recognize this man?

The one in the white shirt, vest and conductor's hat? It may possibly be George L. Colgrove, erstwhile stage coach driver, who made a career jump that added continued years of excitement to his life. He started as 2nd Conductor for South Pacific Coast Railway, and retired as conductor for Southern Pacific.

Letting off some steam at the S.P.C. Railway Station in Los Gatos, is Engine #15. Her crew (and a few family members) stands by. The Los Gatos Hotel (later renamed the Lyndon) can be seen in the background. Photograph, circa 1884, courtesy of William A. Wulf.

The Los Gatos Train Depot, looking north, circa 1900. Note the 3-rail tracks. Obviously, progress was being made on converting the narrow gauge to broad gauge. Note the passengers - men in suits and women in elegant long gowns. In the background, far right, can be seen the Lyndon Livery Stables, and a horse-drawn fire "water pumper" on wheels. Also in the background, far left, can be seen a landmark building, facing on Main Street, still housing businesses today. Photograph courtesy of William A. Wulf.

Adair & Place
Home For Funerals
W. Kent Adair

115 North Santa Cruz Avenue
Los Gatos, California
(408) 354-4122

Above is an artist's rendition of West and East Main Street, near the intersection with North Santa Cruz Avenue, Los Gatos, in the 1890's looking east toward the Main Street Bridge. Beyond are the foothills that form a backdrop for the Blossom Hill area. A train approaches the depot which is just out of sight in front of the Los Gatos Hotel. Below is an advertisement for a business in Los Gatos which served the community for over 90 years - the Adair and Place Home for Funerals, now the Chart House Restaurant. (It took many years for older Los Gatans to accept - if they ever did - this unlikely change in occupancy.)

New power poles at the intersection of Santa Cruz Avenue and Main Street indicate this photograph was taken from the train depot prior to 1900. Out of view at the far left is the Los Gatos Hotel. The Hofstra Block, on the left, was erected in 1893 and is now known as the La Canada Building. It housed the first Telephone Exchange and the IOOF Hall, and was later well known for its Corner Drug Store. Across the street, on the right, was the Theresa Block, constructed in 1891 by John W. Lyndon and named for his wife. It first housed the Bank of Los Gatos and a real estate office, then the Bank of Los Gatos was replaced by the Bank of Italy. It was replaced in 1931, and the new building housed the Bank of America for many years. More recently, The Curious Book Shoppe and other commercial ventures occupied the space when the Bank of America moved to new quarters. The Curious Book Shoppe has now moved further east on Main Street.

A View on Main Street, circa 1920, from the Los Gatos - Saratoga Times Observer, November 12, 1977.

The north side of Main Street, just east of University Avenue, reveals an unpaved roadway, but Coca Cola had arrived (note the sign in the sweet shop window). The Interurban Street Car was still an important mode of transportation, and would be for another 14 years. Obviously, not everyone yet owned an automobile! Bicycles were popular (note the ornate rack the gentlemen is leaning against), and dress was somewhat more casual. One of the stores, Berryman's, at the far right, was eventually torn down; the other three, however, still house businesses today.

Another View on Main Street - The Intersection of East Main and Front Streets.

The imposing newly-built Ford Opera House, on the left, filled a need. Both previous Opera Houses (The Seanor and The Johnson located across the Main Street Bridge between what is today Church Street and High School Court) had been destroyed by fire. The tiled-roof, 2-story building across the street, on the right, displayed an interesting sign:

> ***"Hunts Royal Aztec Tamales" and "Quick Lunch, Hot Coffee, Bread, Cakes, Pies, Cold Drinks, Ice Cream, Candies, Oysters and Catfish."***

Just out of camera range was a large sign printed on the building itself, "Johns and Johnson, Druggists."

The San Jose-Los Gatos Interurban Railway tracks indicate this photograph was taken after 1904, when they were installed, but prior to 1906 when the San Francisco Earthquake reduced the cupolas on the building, left background, to rubble. All of these buildings house interesting and unique businesses today. Photograph courtesy of William A. Wulf.

Busy Intersection - Main Street and Santa Cruz Avenue.

This rare photograph shows all three modes of transportation available in Los Gatos around 1910. The horse-drawn wagon, the "horse-powered" automobile, and the electric powered streetcar, "Big Red." Incidentally, the first automobile, or "horseless carriage," as it was referred to, was seen on the streets of Los Gatos in 1889. Many locals believed it would only be a passing fancy because of all the noise and fumes. Photograph courtesy of William A. Wulf.

Another view on Main Street, circa 1904, from the center of the bridge, looking west.

The San Jose-Los Gatos Interurban Street Car (note the newly installed power poles), was about to take on some Los Gatos passengers. The street was still unpaved, and the sidewalks were wooden, flanked by hitching posts. Horse-drawn wagons and carts used either side of the street, and there was no such offense as jay-walking. In the distance can be seen the spire on the Christian Church (no longer there), and the tower on the La Canada Building, a landmark.

A more modern view of Main Street, taken by the author from the center of the bridge, looking west. The power poles are gone, along with Big Red and the Interurban Street Car tracks, but there are lamp posts. The road is, at long last, paved and the sidewalks are concrete. Many of the same buildings exist, under slightly different guise, ownership and occupancy (note the loss of the cupolas atop the building on the right). The hitching posts are also gone, replaced by a row of shade trees which will no doubt, one day, totally obliterate this view.

Looking east on Main Street.

A rare photograph showing the transitional period between modes of transportation, circa 1910. The horse-drawn cart was eventually replaced by the automobile, as was also the electric street car. Note the street light directly over the oncoming wagon. Photograph courtesy of William A. Wulf.

North Santa Cruz Avenue, looking north, from its intersection with Main Street, circa 1950. And will the owner please call his dog?...

This street developed commercially several years after Main Street, which boasted of the original "downtown" section. The reason for this was, that in the early days (1858 to 1880) it was not on but at right angles to the all-important route from San Jose. There were no other bridges across Los Gatos Creek, as there are today at Saratoga-Los Gatos, and Blossom Hill Roads, making it easily accessible. Today it looks more like Main Street than Main Street itself!

Many of these buildings, although severely damaged during the earthquakes of 1906 and 1989, have been up-dated and retrofitted, and are now occupied by unique shops and restaurants. The tall graceful pine halfway down the left side of the Avenue was planted years ago on the property of the Adair & Place Home for Funerals, now the Chart House Restaurant.

This photograph, taken in 1894, at one of the many photographic studios in San Jose, and reprinted in the Times-Observer, February 16, 1978, shows some early Las Gatans. Standing, on the left, is Mary McMurtry, one of the original founders of the Los Gatos History Club. The other woman standing is unidentified. Seated, left is George McMurtry, and right, Dr. Frank Knowles, one of the first doctors in town. Front, left, is Ella Knowles Yocco. The Yocco family owned a house on Church St. that in the early days became an overnight stopping place for teamsters hauling tan bark to San Jose. And front, right, Kate McMurtry. The McMurtry family owned the first built house in Los Gatos at Main and Church Streets, and also a general store.

Hotel Lyndon Stables.

Fire destroyed the Los Gatos Hotel in 1898. When it rose from the ashes at the southwest corner of Santa Cruz Avenue and Main Street, it was renamed the Lyndon Hotel. Then, after another disastrous fire in 1901 which started in the Lyndon Livery Stables on Front Street across from the train depot, the stables, as seen above were rebuilt in back of the famous hotel.

West Main Street.

There is no trace of these buildings today, which were originally located on West Main Street in back of the Hofstra Block (La Canada Building). After one temporary move, the Christian Church, left, relocated on Daves Avenue, and the feed store, with its lodge accommodations upstairs for the Ancient Order of United Workmen (later a Boy Scout Hall), was torn down in 1930. The site today is a parking lot for the La Canada Building.

Los Gatos Agricultural Works, circa 1870.

This photograph, reprinted in the Times-Observer, is from an original in the Los Gatos Library Collection. The Agricultural Works, a "refined term" for blacksmith shop, was located on East Main Street between Church Street and High School Court. The Works, and the Seanor Opera House next door, were destroyed by fire on October 18, 1890. Pictured are, left to right, John Erickson, Harry Ball, George Seanor, Charles Erickson and James Pierce. Today the site is a parking lot between the Masonic Temple and the Los Gatos-Saratoga Recreation Department Building.

The first elementary through 12th grade school in downtown Los Gatos was housed in a beautiful 2-story Victorian building built in 1875 (resplendent with belfry and "widow's walk"). It was situated on University Avenue, next to Saint Luke's Episcopal Church, on what is now Old Town property. The first graduating class of 1897 was comprised of 10 students. This Victorian served until 1925, when the mission-styled complex that today houses Old Town was built. Elementary classes moved there. Someone once asked. "Why is this street named University Avenue, when there is no university here?" And the reply was "It sounded more prestigious than School Street."

The first Los Gatos High School was built on Main Street in 1908. Later, this building became a part of the present-day school that was built around it in 1925. Finally, this original structure was either swallowed up or torn down by the early 1940's, so that no trace of it remained.

Around the turn of the century, major fires destroyed much of the downtown section on more than one occasion. "There was total destruction along Main Street after the fire of October 13, 1901," according to a newspaper article. "All buildings on both sides of the street from the bridge westward to the railroad tracks were burned to the ground. Fire broke out in the early morning in the rear of a livery stable opposite the Southern Pacific Depot on Front Street."

Another fire, not receiving the same coverage but nevertheless pointing out how quickly things can happen, was reported as "A Close Call":

> *"Just a few minutes before the funeral procession of Mr. Day, on last Tuesday afternoon, reached the Episcopal Church, the Christmas decorations which had not been taken down, caught on fire from a gas jet, and in an instant were a mass of flames. Dr. Urquhart and Jas. Gray, who were standing near, and at the risk of being burned severely, grabbed the fiery mass and carried it out of the building. If it hadn't been for them the church would surely have been consumed."*

Fires were not the only calamity to plague Los Gatos in the early days. The first Main Street Bridge over Los Gatos Creek, with its steep pulls on either side to get back up to road level, was built in 1858. It was destroyed in the flood of 1862. Almost the same fate awaited its replacement 10 years later in 1872. Both of these bridges, which had the appearance of railroad trestles, were replaced in 1882 by a single-arched wooden span bridge. This one lasted until 1906. All of these structures were built and paid for by Santa Clara County, as there still was no town officially established at this time. As mentioned earlier, Los Gatos was incorporated in 1887.

As so often happens, each fire and flood tended only to improve and modernize the town. In 1906, the Town of Los Gatos and the San Jose-Los Gatos Interurban Railway Company, each paid half to build a three-arch, stone-faced concrete bridge at this site, which stood until 1955 when it was replaced by the present concrete bridge over Highway 17.

A few years earlier, in 1902, according to William A. Wulf, Mr. and Mrs. Theodore J. Morris returned to the Los Gatos area after spending thirty years in the Orient, where Mr. Morris worked for the China-Japan Trading Company. On property they purchased midway along the Los Gatos-Saratoga Road, across from the intersection with Quito Road, they built their gracious Nippon Mura, which, when translated, means "Japanese Village." Their Torii Tea Room and exquisite Oriental gardens gained popularity and drew people from miles around. Today, it is known as La Hacienda Inn. In spite of the Spanish name, evidence of the original Japanese architecture is still visible, and patrons continue to come great distances to enjoy the continental cuisine and restful atmosphere.

After several frustrating starts, the San Jose-Los Gatos Interurban Railway was established following an 18-mile-route that took it from San Jose through Campbell, Los Gatos, Saratoga and back to San Jose, via Meridian Corners. Out of Saratoga there was a spur line that ran up to Congress Springs, a popular resort.

Congress Springs.

This exciting, elegant and fashionable mineral spa and health resort was located in the foothills above Saratoga. It was originally built in 1866 and consisted of 14 rooms. From Miss Cunningham's book, SARATOGA'S FIRST HUNDRED YEARS, "The Hotel, with its spacious main building and broad veranda was situated on a protected plateau of the mountainside with a spectacular view of heavily timbered hills. Shade trees, extensive lawns and rare tropical flowers surrounded the buildings. The average rates were $ 2.50 a day for room and board, or $ 10.00 to $ 15.00 per week. The surrounding hills were filled with quail, dove, rabbits and squirrels, and Saratoga Creek, which ran through the resort, was a fine trout stream."

The hotel sold in 1872 to Lewis P. Sage and his son for approximately $ 25,000.00. By 1881 they had expanded the facility to 63 rooms with surrounding cottages. But it was the mineral springs that continued to draw clientele, for years, including many internationally famous people, until a major fire reduced this entire complex to ashes.

The electric trolley cars were inaugurated in 1904. Standard gauge, operating from 600-volt overhead lines, the little railway cars made hourly runs. Mrs. Dora Rankin recalled in her earlier memoirs:

> *"About the biggest excitement in town (Los Gatos) since the fire was when the Interurban tracks were laid and the cars began to run. Now we could go to San Jose or Congress Springs whenever we wanted to.*
>
> *"Congress Springs was a beautiful recreation park with a dance platform, a ballpark and a pretty lake where we could go for a boat or raft ride. There was a walk leading up to the springs where we added lemon juice to the natural soda water, making what we thought was a wonderful drink."*

According to John Baggerly's article on the Interurban Cars which appeared in the Los Gatos Times Observer, April 2, 1985, shoppers and commuters found them convenient; high school students found them secluded trysting spots; "rowdies" found them excellent get-away vehicles after coming into town to harass the local boys; and one man, so the story goes, even found his Maker, when a car jumped the tracks at the corner of Saratoga and North Santa Cruz Avenues and plowed right into the little cemetery!

After 1909, according to William Wulf, the system was called the Peninsular Railway, and in 1910 the original "Pullman Green" color of the cars was replaced by Chinese Red, hence the later nickname "Red Cars." Then, after fifteen years, in 1925 the Interurban Cars were painted once again, this time two-tone - apple green below the windows, and light creme above. For over 25 years before finally giving way to progress in the form of the automobile, these cars played an important role in the transportation of passengers around the Santa Clara Valley.

The climate of this area had been likened to Assouan, Egypt, a city on the Nile, which was considered by many world travelers to be the most perfect on earth. This news brought an influx of people suffering from rheumatism, consumption, and asthma. On a more positive note, writers, artists, entertainers, and inventors also came, seeking the quiet tranquillity and inspiration found in the foothills. By 1906, Los Gatos was well supplied with hotels, restaurants, and boarding houses. There were two large first class sixty-room hotels, the Lyndon and the El Monte, and these were reinforced by two good smaller ones, the Los Gatos and the Olympia.

Jack London and John Steinbeck did much of their best writing here. According to an article by James P. Delgado printed in the Time-Observer, June 15, 1978: Because they were plagued with curious on-lookers, tourists in their yard, and even Peeping Toms at their windows, Steinbeck and his wife, Carol, decided to move. They left their beloved 2-acre "Arrojo de Ajo" (Garlic Gulch) on Greenwood Avenue in Los Gatos for a more secluded spot. They settled on larger acreage up near Montezuma School on Black Road. Here, at last, the great John Steinbeck was able to finish his manuscript, THE GRAPES OF WRATH, in relative peace and quiet.

Actress/sisters Olivia de Havilland and Joan Fontaine both attended Los Gatos High School, and their famous mother, Lilian Fontaine, was well known for her work in the theater. She produced many plays and extravaganzas, one of her most famous being, "A Midsummer's Night's Dream." At Villa Montalvo, an estate once owned by the late Senator James D. Phelan, there is an outdoor amphitheater for the performing arts named in her honor.

Mark Twain paid a visit to his good friend Josephine McCracken up on the summit, and back downtown in Los Gatos a certain Mr. Macabee drew out his plans and developed what was to become about the best darn gopher trap in the country!

Los Gatos was a popular jumping-off point to go other places like the beaches in Santa Cruz, the Fishermans Wharf and still-embryonic Cannery Row in Monterey, and all the still popular mountain resorts. The excursion trains were always crowded. Garten Keyston, an early resident, also recalled the sportsmen's trains which departed town late on Sunday afternoons. They were bound for several mountain lodges, and the cars were filled with jovial hunters, guns, and whining, anxious dogs.

Now that Los Gatos, "Gem of the Foothills", was on the verge of an unbelievable period of growth, could the land developers be far behind?

Correction: The fire of 1901 did not start in the livery stable, as initial newspaper reports indicated, according to historian William A. Wulf, but rather in a French Bakery on Park Street. From there the fire burned westward on both sides of Main Street all the way to the railroad tracks, sparing only the Station. The track area fortunately acted as a fire break, halting the forward progress of the flames.

> *Little Willie Turner, the one who went to God, died at the age of three after complications from relatively simple orthopedic surgery. Another mystery solved.*

The Los Gatos Mail, Thursday April 5, 1906:

"If you desire to abolish saloons in Los Gatos, vote NO on the question: Shall the sale of liquor be licensed? If you wish saloons to continue, vote YES. Isn't that plain? Vote NO!"

Pam Tobari wrote in a 1984 newspaper article about the life of Ida Berti Cavallini, a local Los Gatos resident. Ida was celebrating her 90th birthday and recalling the early days, "Life was simpler, but not necessarily easier."

CHAPTER 34

THE GREAT EARTHQUAKE AND FIRE OF 1906

Very early in the morning of April 18, 1906, at the St. Francis Hotel in San Francisco, Enrico Caruso, the famous operatic tenor, was still basking in dreams of glory. His nine standing ovations, at the conclusion of "Carmen" a few hours earlier, foretold of a good run. Elsewhere, railroad crews were getting ready to go about their business. A construction train was preparing to start its daily routine of removing old and installing new track and ballasting it up. The Chinese were assembling their work crews and chattering amongst themselves. An engine had just filled up with water from the newly erected water tank at Newark, on the Oakland side of the Bay, and had chugged back to its waiting cars. Other engines were working up heads of steam in Alameda and Los Gatos, and the station agent at Laurel had just returned from Wrights on a hand car. It was hard pumping as he had been 'celebrating' most of the night at a dance at Wrights Hotel...

Along California's San Andreas Fault, (a weakened 650-mile-long swath through the earth's crust running both above and below sea level) a massive shift was about to take place. It was to claim the lives of hundreds of people, affect the lives of thousands more, and change the course of California history.

At 5:13 A.M. an ominous rumbling preceded the major shock wave. Then suddenly, violent movement of rock masses 20 to 30 miles below ground's surface (twice the depth of most seismic activity), created devastating forces which emanated north and south along the fault line just west of Santa Rosa. Simultaneously, shock waves reaching 8.3 on the Richter Scale swept out from the epicenter in ever-widening circles. Other fault lines running parallel to and off of the San Andreas shuddered in sympathy. (The Richter Magnitude Scale was not published until 1935 but, according to Robert Iacopi in his book EARTHQUAKE COUNTRY, records have made it possible to go back several years and assign magnitudes to prior major earthquakes.)

The violent temblor, moving earth both vertically and horizontally at the same time, leveled the town of Santa Rosa. Within seconds it wrecked havoc in San Francisco where brick and mortar ground together and buildings crumbled. Many people were killed by the collapsing walls and falling masonry off the ornate Victorian-style structures. The acrid smell of dust and debris filled the air.

Water mains were among the hardest hit initial casualties. While the water lines throughout the city spewed their liquid uselessly into the air, gas mains were severed and fires erupted, compounding the physical damage, with no way of fighting them.

Across the San Francisco Bay, the new steel water tank along the railroad siding in Newark, buckled and crashed to the tracks below wasting thousands more gallons of water. Further away, the San Jose business district suffered major structural damage. (What was left standing, in many instances, was so fractured that it had to be torn down later.) And near Palo Alto, Stanford University saw several of its most beautiful buildings, like its entrance way, domed library, and Memorial Church, reduced to rubble.

In the mountains of the Coastal Range, the two longest tunnels on the narrow gauge line, from Wrights to Laurel and Laurel to Glenwood, suffered massive damage both inside and out as the ceilings caved in. Tons of earth and rock then slid down over the portals, sealing them off. The track which once entered the tunnel at Wrights was off-set by 3 to 4 feet. Steel track along other sections of the route popped loose, and was bent and twisted into odd metal sculptures.

Excerpts from newspaper accounts on the 19th and 26th of April pinpoint some of the other local damage:

"From all reports the higher altitudes of the Santa Cruz Mountains, all the way from beyond Saratoga to Loma Prieta on both slopes, appear to have been more seriously disturbed than many locations in the valleys and foothills. In many places the roads are impassable not only on account of great avalanches of stones and earth but of wide and deep cracks in the earth where the ground was rent asunder."

"Mountain springs dried up, and trees were bent from the vertical to crazy angles. Neatly planted rows of fruit trees were out of alignment. In the Chemeketa Park area above Los Gatos, a large acreage of young firs slanted towards the east."

"Above hard-hit Alma, fissures were opened in a hundred places of from a few inches to three feet in width. The depth of these is not apparent, as the ground is broken in a zig-zag manner."

Near the summit and present-day Highway 17, *"The earthquake ruptured a dirt road in front of a blacksmith's shop. Nearby, a house was torn in two when fault opened directly beneath it."*

"A slide on the banks of the Los Gatos Creek at Eva, midway between Alma and Wrights, interfered with the flow of water, and it backed up making a small sized lake which in places attained a depth of from 50 to 100 feet."

"Acres of ground came down the mountainside, obliterating all of Hoffman's Shingle Mill off Reservoir Road at the head of Little Deer Creek. Two men lost their lives."

"The Rhodes oil well on which thousands of dollars had been spent in boring, without any encouragement in the shape of oil, is now reported to be showing oil in quantities. The oil wells in Moody's Gulch discharged oil for days after the quake at the rate of 50 to 100 barrels per day, which ran down the gulch and emptied into the creek."

"Los Gatos was visited by an earthquake and this was followed by others at intervals until this morning. There was considerable damage to merchants and buildings."

Dora Rankin recalled in her childhood memories of Los Gatos:

"The kitchen floor was a mass of bricks and plaster and broken beams, and everything on the pantry shelves was in a pile on the floor. The chimney over the back parlor looked as if it had been cut and twisted around. All week long, the ground shook and trembled at intervals..."

At Santa Cruz, reports came in of *"tidal waves and awful destruction"*, but much of this proved to be without truth. Damage here was comparable to that in Los Gatos. An eerie place, later called "Crazy Forest" by the local residents, was created at the headwaters of Soquel Creek by the disruptive forces. Trees fell and were laid out in all different directions, and a lake formed that lasted several years. An effort was made to preserve the area for historical purposes but state money went instead to repair Highway 1.

Back in San Francisco, friends of the opera and members of the cast were alarmed when Enrico did not show up in the lobby of the St. Francis. When they broke into his room they found him clinging to his bedpost and weeping uncontrollably.

According to a newspaper story by Patricia Loomis, printed in retrospect on April 18, 1980, honoring the hero of the day of the "Great Earthquake and Fire":

By 6:30 A.M. in San Francisco, an hour after the initial quake, Brig. General Frederick Funston, Commanding Officer of the Presidio, took some immediate steps to stem the tide of destruction by fire. Without going through proper channels (in other words, the mayor, whom he was at odds with anyway, and other city officials) he placed San Francisco under military control. He called up troops from Angel Island, marines from Mare Island, and more soldiers from Fort Baker on Alcatraz and the Presidio in Monterey. He also called on the mayor of Oakland to "send engines, hose and dynamite immediately", and the mayor of San Francisco concurred, realizing it was not the time for petty bickering.

The arriving military personnel set to work assisting and guarding the people of the city and establishing temporary shelters on the grounds of the Presidio, at Golden Gate Park and other sites. They were ordered to shoot to kill any looters or perpetrators of other crimes and not an insignificant number lost their lives in this fashion.

Funston felt that dynamite was the only means of defense against the fire, establishing a "fire break" of sorts. Blasting began the next day on Van Ness Avenue, and could be heard for 50 miles, as far away as San Jose. Meanwhile, refugees huddled in the make-shift camps fighting such continuing problems as contaminated water and outbreaks of measles, smallpox, and scarlet fever.

In a news article by Bill Strobel, published on April 18, 1978 on the 72nd anniversary of the devastating quake, he recaps the headlines of that awful day:

"SAN FRANCISCO IN RUINS; 600 - 700 DEAD; 28,000 BUILDINGS DESTROYED; 225,000 HOMELESS."

Caruso, who was still trying to get out of the city two days after the quake, was sure he had lost his voice through fright and stress. He supposedly cried with a vengeance, once aboard the launch that would take him to the safety of Oakland, *"Give me Vesuvio, but NO more San Francisco!"*

Most of the 75,000 square miles that shook so violently for 28 seconds were uninhabited in 1906. But that pronouncement would have been of little consolation to those immediately affected on that fateful April morning.

Alice Greeg, a survivor, sat on the stoop of her narrow but still-upright Victorian hillside home. She wrote in a letter to her cousin back East as she viewed the scene before her:

"Ruin...

Ruin

Ruin... for miles around. It is inconceivable to me..."

San Francisco City Hall, once an elegant landmark, was devastated by the 5:12 a.m. massive earthquake on that fateful April 18th in 1906. The tower collapsed during the initial jolts, and the walls caved in. The coup de grace came in the form of fire which burned through the rubble until only this skeleton was left. Photograph is from the California Division of Mines collection.

The earth shook both horizontally and vertically at the same time. Because of the hilly topography and poor earth compaction in many parts of San Francisco, streets (mostly brick) were laid open by gaping fissures, and sidewalks and cablecar tracks twisted in sympathy. Photograph is from the California Palace of the Legion of Honor.

The *beautiful sandstone entrance arches on Palm Drive, Stanford University Campus (30 miles south of San Francisco), were standing like sentinels one moment and reduced to piles of rubble the next. Also heavily damaged was Stanford's Memorial Church. The entire face of the building, done in intricate tile mosaics, came crashing down, as well as many of the long rows of arches which encircled the rest of the Quad. Stanford Direction October 1977.*

954 Ashbury Street,
San Francisco, Cal.
February 1, 1920.

Brother Roland T. Meacham,
Convention Manager,
Cleveland, Ohio.

My Dear Brother Meacham:-

I have just received your very kind and very pressing invitation to attend the Eighty-sixth-eighty-eighth Convention of Alpha Delta Phi. I have received previous invitations - many of them begging me to come, or at least send ten dollars, which I have undutifully failed to acknowledge. But a real, honest-to-goodness invitation, not mimeographed, and signed by the Convention Manager his own self, cannot be ignored.

I note you are getting letters from the older brethren expressing "unfeigned regret" that they are unable to attend by reason of "the infirmities of age." I cannot attend the convention, but I will be hanged if that is because of the infirmities of age or any other infirmity. Not by a jugful! It is because I am too infernally busy. I am doing more work than I ever did until recently, more, in fact, than it is decent to ask any man to do who is not a Captain of Industry or an oil stock promoter, eating three square meals every day and getting no end of fun out of life.

I have today written four editorials -- all solid chuncks of wisdom, cleaned out my chicken house, worked an hour in my shop because it was raining so that I could not work in the garden, balanced my little bank account which never takes less than two hours, which is rough for a chap who led the class of 1860 in mathematics as long as he stayed with it - and am writing this while waiting for dinner.

I write from three to five editorials a day, edit two pages of agricultural stuff for the weekly Chronicle, write a financial or economic monograph for the financial page of the Chronicle every Monday, write a financial letter for one of our largest banks every month, contribute to the high cost of living by running a prune farm 60 miles away, and can brag in a blatant fashion that is absolutely shameless as you observe.

A letter written by Edward F. Adams to brother Roland T. Meacham, convention manager of the Eighty-Sixth - Eighty-Eighth Convention of the Alpha Delta Phi Fraternity. Adams was unable to attend, not because of his age (80 years) or infirmities or even lack of funds like many of his fraternal brothers but, true to form, because he was just too infernally busy!

Mr. Roland T. Meacham, page #2

As my friend and brother Alpha Delt, President Emeritus Benjamin Ide Wheeler, has been good enough to mention the recent celebration of what, out here, they call my "first eightieth birthday", by an important civic organization which he and I helped to get going, I am sending you under separate cover a copy of the proceedings which I had reported in order that I might gratify my vanity by sending copies whenever I can make an excuse to do so. It is adorned, as you will see, with a similitude of myself equipped with a mighty knife wherewithall I am about to mobilize against a tremendous cake. When it has served whatever purpose it may before or during the coming convention, I beg that it be turned over to Hudson Chapter to repose in its archives - or its waste basket as may seem most appropriate.

I observe that you suggest that I respond with the expression of some lofty sentiment such as might be reasonably expected from a wise but doddering old gentleman. Bless my soul, my dear boys, you are not assembled to absorb wisdom, but to have a good time, and that you may do so is the sincere wish of,

Yours in cordial and fraternal regard,

Edward F. Adams
Hudson 1860.

Check for $10.00 enclosed towards expenses.
EFA/MR

EPILOGUE

Eventually, the dust did settle. And over the years and out of the ashes and rubble that once was San Francisco emerged a bustling more metropolitan city, certainly one with more stringent building and fire codes. The construction trades boomed, but, unfortunately, gone was the pioneering spirit and the satisfaction that comes from tackling a problem and solving it for the very first time, except for one epic achievement - The Panama-Pacific International Exhibition. Skeptics said the grandiose plan could never be accomplished within the time frame, especially with so much earthquake devastation to deal with. But San Franciscan's proved them wrong and everyone was extremely proud of this achievement, held in honor of the opening of the Panama Canal in 1915.

After the earthquake, it took three years to repair the railway system over the Santa Cruz Mountains. But this gave Southern Pacific ample time to install that critical third rail to turn the line - at long last - into broad gauge. Thirty years later, however, saw the end of the era. Even if the trains were packed with passengers and freight (which they were not) it was simply not a money-making proposition. World War I, followed by a staggering economic depression felt around the globe, and competition from the automobile and trucking industries, followed by yet another World War, were the deciding factors in many a death knell. The line from Los Gatos to Santa Cruz was closed down with the passing of the last train through the mountains on March 4, 1940. The tracks were dismantled and then ripped out, and the infernal tunnels were blasted shut once and for all. At the beginning of the Second World War, local residents, it was reported, blasted the Wrights end of the Summit Tunnel with dynamite themselves to seal it off for fear of "enemy infiltration." The tunnel at Zayante, however, escaped the same fate. Instead, it was used for storage of important and classified documents during the war years.

Mountain Charley McKiernan lost a nine year old son in a shooting incident when a gun the child was playing with at home went off accidentally. McKiernan, grief-stricken, never fully recovered from this tragedy. He eventually moved his family down to San Jose, as he wanted his surviving children to have easier access to high school and college. Although he continued to maintain his mountain property holdings, he adjusted to his new surroundings and started several businesses and belonged to many organizations. He was an active Mason, and was a member of two Lodges - Number 10 in San Jose, and Number 38 in Santa Cruz. He seemed invincible, this fiery Irishman of strong will and mind and body but in 1892 he became ill and passed away a short time later. His first famous mountain cabin was destroyed by fire, although, at the summit today, one of his other log cabins is still standing. The memory of Charley McKiernan lingers on.

George L. Colgrove was a man of true integrity. He loved Los Gatos and the Santa Cruz Mountains and would have gladly settled there except for the fact that his wife preferred Oakland and the cool Bay breezes. He worked 36 years, 1 month and 8 days for the Southern Pacific Railway. He was never discharged or even laid off, and he never missed a day of pay or had a grievance before the Company (although a couple of times he was a little disgusted). Probably the worst offense he ever committed was to lie about his age. Company policy dictated he should have retired at age 70 but (and this is where the Great Earthquake and Fire of 1906 actually worked in someone's favor) all the Company records had been consumed by flames. When asked his vital statistics, in order to reconstitute the personnel files, he conveniently changed his date of birth. He loved the railroad that much! And Conductor Colgrove retired - finally - at the age of 73, with not many the wiser.

For one brief moment in time, according to John V. Young in his book GHOST TOWNS OF THE SANTA CRUZ MOUNTAINS, a political/religious zealot, by the name of William E. Riker flashed across the sky like a blazing meteor. He founded a community just above the Lexington area which he called Holy City. Here, Father Riker had all the intentions of establishing the seat of "The World's Most Perfect Government" and, for a time, impressionable people flocked to the site. The town took on a garish look, boasting a restaurant, gas station, "observatory" with huge telescopes, radio station, newspaper office and outlandish billboards. But followers eventually became disenchanted with the rantings of Father Riker on such topics as "white supremacy, communal living and total abstinence" and drifted away. The final blow came when a realignment of Highway 17 took the lines of cars and visitors off in another direction. Perhaps the world was just not ready for such a Mecca as Holy City.

New railroads and interstate highways for automobiles and trucks now allowed people the opportunity to travel further and further from home. Instead of going to the little mountain park above Los Gatos, the one festooned with gay Japanese lanterns, people could visit Yosemite, Lake Tahoe and even Hollywood! Sadly, the mountain resorts were on the wane.

But as the mountain towns died, the valley and coastal towns grew. Work had started on Highway 5, connecting Los Gatos and Santa Cruz, and the cutting and widening was completed by 1919. Two years later, the road was "Set in Concrete" (quite a thick layer, too, because of the heavy loads it still bore). According to a notation under a photograph hanging in the Los Gatos Public Library, "The road paralleled the Southern Pacific tracks on a good part of the journey." In 1939, as the road was replaced with 4 lanes, and renamed Highway 17, it lost some of its curves and by-passed most of the scenic and historic communities that had made this particular 20-mile gap so interesting.

The communities of Lexington and Alma, along with the vast surrounding meadow at the entrance to those beautiful "Blue Mountains" disappeared under water. The basin was dammed above Los Gatos and a reservoir, known as Lake Lexington, was created in 1952. Mary Main of Los Gatos, who grew up in Lexington, spoke fondly of her mountain home. "It was the most beautiful thing in the world, our 175 acres," (between Black and Bear Creek Roads) "and our house had 22 bedrooms," (to amply accommodate the large family of adults and a dozen children). In 1951, the county put a value on the few still-existing properties, and paid off the homeowners. Most of the homes were torn down although a few owners opted to be moved to higher ground. Mary Main never got over what happened. "I hate the thing that destroyed our place; it makes me cry whenever I go by," she said sadly.

Between the hunters and the determined farmers and ranchers, trying to establish themselves and protect their livestock, the wild game population began to dwindle. Fortunately, some animals were able to slink away. They migrated to the southern and northern most uninhabited reaches of the Coastal Range, and as far away as the High Sierra. By the late 1800's there was hardly a bear or mountain lion to be found. "The wild is fast disappearing, man is paving over, building on, mining, lumbering and cultivating former feeding lands. There's relatively little roaming space for wildlife left..."

Starting in the 1950's meetings and heated discussions about turning Highway 17 into a multi-lane freeway were commonplace. One would be hard pressed to find a mountain resident, though, willing to give up his land or stand of redwood trees to such a project, and Santa Cruz was equally adamant about not wanting thousands upon thousands of cars pouring into its city limits in search of the beach and boardwalk. In the first place, there was no parking... There were also attempts in the 1960s and 70s to re-establish the train system over the Santa Cruz Mountains from a tourist attraction point of view. To date the results of this effort have not been successful but there are still plans on the drawing board.

Another earthquake of epic proportions (7.2 on the Richter Scale) emanated from near the peak of Loma Prieta in the Santa Cruz Mountains on October 17, 1989. It shook and rumbled up an down the San Andreas Fault, frightening people for hundreds of miles around, especially those who had gathered to watch the World Series opener at Candlestick Park in South San Francisco, and with good reason. Many lives were lost when double deck freeway sections collapsed in Oakland, a portion of the lower level of the Bay Bridge also collapsed, and a fire erupted in the Marina District of San Francisco, while skyscrapers swayed ominously. And further south, close to the epicenter, major damage had occurred in the quaint towns of Los Gatos and Santa Cruz, some of which is still evident today...

As many wise men have suggested, in order to appreciate the present, and perhaps even predict the future, it is necessary to understand the past.

Daniel Webster once said,
"Regarding our ability to hold communion with our ancestors, we become their contemporaries, live the lives they lived, endure what they endured and partake of the rewards which they enjoyed."

Kids used to cut through the Summit tunnel, especially the Laurel to Glenwood bore. It was almost a full day's trip over the surface - through the wild lilac, chaparral, madrone, and that awful pesky poison oak - so, as dangerous as the practice was, kids did it to save time.

April 19, 1906

One day after the massive earthquake wrecked havoc along portions of the mountain route, a most amazing story came to light. George Crall, Los Gatos resident and merchant decided to see if he could get to Santa Cruz. He was, according to William A. Wulf, able to make it as far as Wrights where the train's forward progress came to a halt. The tunnel had caved in and would remain closed to through traffic for the next three years. The spunky Mr. Crall, however, determined to complete what he set out to do, hiked over the mountain and down into Laurel. There he found the Laurel to Glenwood Tunnel still passable, and tempting fate, cut through it on foot! He was lucky - it, too, collapsed within the week after high magnitude aftershocks finished it off. But there in Glenwood was the first train out of Santa Cruz, puffing steam, and waiting to make the return run. Mr. Crall took this picture to prove his story. Photograph courtesy of William A. Wulf.

The Little Town of Alma in 1910

In its heyday, Alma was an important stage coach stop, later lumbermills site, and, starting in the 1880's, South Pacific Coast's bustling train stop. By 1910, the echoes of Buffalo Jones' had died, along with the needs of everything save the train. But in 1906 the major earthquake even took some of that importance away. Although the rail system was closed to over-the mountain through traffic until 1909 because the tunnels were under reconstruction, the local train out of Los Gatos was still able to run up the mountain as far as Wrights, picking up and delivering school children and other commuters. Photograph courtesy of William A. Wulf.

The commemorative envelope, above, graphically depicts the fate of the small mountain town of Alma, along with its neighboring community of Lexington. Coming down out of the mountains, Los Gatos Creek emptied into this little "punchbowl" area. What better site for a reservoir? Today, with the railway gone and houses and stores torn down or moved to higher ground by Santa Clara County, "Lexington Reservoir occupies the space formerly taken by these two little communities." This commemorative envelop was made available through the late Father William Abeloe, recognized historian and author.

Bridal Vail **Yosemite** **Vernal** **Nevada**

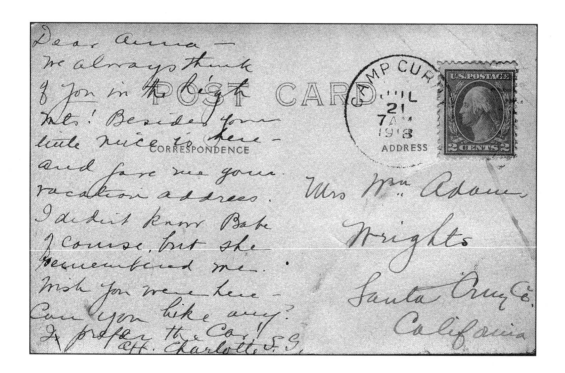

A post card to one of the Adams' family showing some of the breathtaking tourist attractions at Yosemite Park. Courtesy of Frank Adams.

Recipes Of The Era

The following selection of recipes reflects the times, and the varied tastes of the many nationalities depicted in the text. The recipes have been up-dated only to make them easier to read. Basically, they contain the same ingredients and methods as originally written. Some recipes indicate no length of time for cooking. It's the authors' conclusion that Grandma Bascom and Josie Reece just figured we'd know how long to bake a cake.

A list of the 38 recipes follows:

Mince Meat for Pies (English)
Short Pastry
Wu Tung Ling's Chinese Fritters
Beef Pastie Pie (Welch)
Panoche (Mexican Candy)
Beef and Beans (Mexican)
Oil Dressing (Mexican)
Grits to Samp (Indian)
Gnocchi (Italian)
Frosting for Burnt Sugar Cake
Wiener Schnitzel (German/Austrian)
Boiled Coffee
Mexican Flan
French Lace Cookies
Sliced Tomato Salad Au Gratin
To Melt Butter
Coffee Ice Cream
Left-Over Coffee
Coffee Cake

Six-Egg Cake
Sweet Potato Pie
Indian Corn Cakes
Molasses Drop Cakes
Barbecued Pork Tenderloins
Spanish Beans
Suculento (Mexican)
Beans in a Casserole (Spanish)
Josie Reece's Burnt Sugar Cake
Hot Pot Irish Stew
Scotch Short Bread
Hot Chocolate (Mexican)
Stuffed Baked Potatoes
Prune Whip
Gendarme Potatoes
Shallot Vinegar
Harlequin Conserve
Corn Bread
Scripture Cake

Swift's Silver=Leaf Lard

THE WORLD'S STANDARD FOR EXCELLENCE IN SHORTENINGS

Crisp, Flaky Pie Crust

might be called Silver-Leaf pie-crust, its flakiness depends so much on the use of Silver-Leaf Lard in mixing.

Silver-Leaf Lard

will help make your reputation as a pie baker.
For sale in Tins by

Grocers and Markets Generally

The World's Standard for Excellence

Mince Meat for Pies

(Quantity - 4 gallons, plus)

Select a medium size bowl.

To measure take:

5 bowls of apples (peeled, cored and chopped)
5 bowls of sugar
2 bowls of raisins
1 bowl of currants
1 bowl of molasses
1 bowl of vinegar
1 bowl of butter
1 bowl of cider (put in raisins and boil until raisins are soft; add juice and all
3 bowls tender cooked meat (boiled beef, chopped fine)
1 bowl suet, chopped fine
2 Tbsp. each cinnamon, nutmeg, cloves, black pepper, and salt

Cook all ingredients together in a large pot until well flavored. Seal in sterilized jars. If you like, add some brandy or Port wine just before sealing. Store in a cool place. It improves with age.

Six-Egg Cake

One pound of butter beaten to a cream
One pound and a quarter of flour
One pound of fine sugar beat fine
One pound of currants, clean washed and picked
Quarter of an ounce of mace
Quarter of an ounce of ground coriander
Six eggs, two whites left out, beaten well

Mix the flour, sugar and eggs by degrees into the creamed butter, add currents and spices, beat it all well with both hands. Either make it into little cakes or bake it as one.

Ladies Handmaid - 1758 (p. 403)

Short Pastry

3 cups flour
1 level tsp. salt
2 level tsp. baking powder
1 cup shortening
Ice-cold water to mix

In making pastry, the best results are obtained by having all the ingredients and utensils as cold as possible, and keeping them so until the pastry goes into the oven.

*Sift together the flour, salt and baking powder; work in the shortening lightly with the fingers, mix to a firm dough with the ice-cold water and roll out once on a floured board.
Use for whatever purpose desired.*

Sweet Potato Pie

1-1/2 cups mashed cooked sweet potatoes
1/2 cup firmly packed brown sugar
1 tsp. ground cinnamon
1/2 tsp. ground allspice
1/4 tsp. ground mace
3/4 tsp. salt
2 eggs, beaten
1 can (14-1/2 oz.) undiluted evaporated milk
2 Tbsp. butter, melted
1 9" unbaked pie crust, rolled to 1/8"

*Mix all ingredients together and spoon into unbaked pie shell. Bake in preheated hot oven (425 deg.) for 10 minutes.
Reduce heat to 350 deg. and bake 25 minutes longer or until set.
Cool before serving. Top with whipped cream.*

Wu Tung Ling's Fritters

Two cups rice flour, one-half cup sugar

Scald him with hot water, mix him like bread, roll him into balls, put him in hot fat on stove, cook him like doughnuts.

Indian Corn Cakes

Mix a quart of Indian meal with a handful of wheat flour; stir in a quart of warm milk, a tsp. of salt, and two tsp. of yeast; stir alternately into the milk, the meal and 3 well-beaten eggs. When light, bake as buckwheat cakes, on a griddle. Send them to the table hot, with butter and maple syrup.

Beef Pastie Pie (4 Pasties)

2 large raw potatoes, cubed in small pieces
1/2 lb. cubed sirloin steak
4 small turnips, cubed
2 yellow onions, sliced
Fresh parsley, chopped
Salt and pepper
Light cream

Roll out an 8" pie crust circle for each pastie. On each circle, starting at the midline and working toward the edge place a layer of potatoes, a layer of meat, a layer of turnips, a layer of onions, chopped parsley, salt and pepper.

Fold other half of pie crust over the top and seal or crimp the edges as you would a pie. Put slits in the top. Pour a little light cream through the slits. Place on a cookie sheet and bake in the oven at 350 deg. After the first half hour, add 2 to 3 Tbsp. water through holes in the top. Continue baking another half hour until done and pie crust is golden brown. ...One pastie pie per customer, two if you're a miner.

A Welch favorite and an important part of a miner's diet. The pasties were shaped into half circles in order to fit into a special storage area at the bottom of the miner's lantern. Here they could be kept warm until lunch time, and while being eaten could, in turn, warm up a miner's cold hands.

E. G. SKINNER

Keeps always on hand a large and fine assortment
of

Candies, and Delicious Ice Cream,

Special attention given to Family Orders
and Entertainments. Give us a trial.

CAMARILLO, CAL.

General Blacksmithing Horse Shoeing and Machine Work

Automobile Repairing Done Quickly
and Satisfactorily.

Repairing of Windmills of All Kinds.

Come and Give Us a Trial
Satisfaction Guaranteed   **WALTER BELL, Camarillo**

CAMARILLO'S TONSORIAL ARTIST

Can put a new face on your husbands and sweethearts, or shave the one they have. Special attention given to big heads, sore heads and bald heads. A decided improvement in their disappearance guaranteed or money refunded.

ED. RICHARDSON, Camarillo, Cal.

does the work neatly and quickly.

Molasses Drop Cakes

1 cup molasses
1 cup hot water
1/4 cup butter, melted
1 egg
1 tsp. baking soda
1/2 tsp. salt
Flour

Beat together molasses and soda, then add the egg beaten, shortening, salt and water. When thoroughly mixed, add enough flour to make rather thick batter. Drop spoonfuls around in greased pans. Bake in quick oven.

Panoche (Mexican Candy)

Three cups brown sugar, two-thirds cup sweet milk, butter half the size of an egg, one cup walnuts or almonds chopped fine.

Cook the candy till brittle when dropped in cold water. Stir all the time, then add the nuts. Pour out and cool.

Barbecued Pork Tenderloins (Chinese)

1/4 cup soy sauce
2 Tbsp. dry sherry
1 Tbsp. brown sugar
1 Tbsp. honey
1 clove garlic, minced
1/2 tsp. ground cinnamon
2 pork tenderloin strips

Combine the first 6 ingredients. Coat the tenderloins and marinate for 1 or more hours in refrigerator, turning the strips occasionally.
Drain meat saving the marinade. Cook tenderloins on rack over drip pan 45 minutes or until done in 350 deg. oven, turning and basting often. Remove and cool. Slice on the diagonal. Garnish with cilantro (Chinese parsley).

Beef and Beans (Mexican)

- 1 lb. country sausage, ground
- 1 lb. cooked pot or chuck roast, shredded or cubed
- 1 onion, chopped
- 1 clove garlic, minced
- 1 medium green bell pepper, chopped
- 1 medium red sweet pepper, chopped
- 1 large can whole peeled tomatoes, juice and all
- 2 16 oz. cans red kidney beans
- 1 Tbsp. chili powder
- 1/2 tsp. cayenne, or more to taste
  or 1, 2, or 3 fresh jalapeno peppers sliced and seeded (depending on hotness desired)
- 1 cup chicken broth
- 1 tsp. sugar
- 2 tsp. ground cumin
- 1/2 tsp. salt
- Pepper to taste

Crumble and saute sausage with onions, garlic, and green and red peppers in a heavy Dutch oven until browned. Drain off any grease. Add the cubed or shredded cooked beef and the remaining ingredients. Chop up the tomatoes. Cover and simmer for 1-1/2 to 2 hours. Add water as needed. Sprinkle each serving with cilantro leaves. Serves 8.

Spanish Beans

Soak three pints of pink beans over night. Next day, boil the beans with a little baking soda. Then pour off water and add fresh cold water, and one pint of canned tomatoes. Scrape out centers of four ripe chili peppers, chop in small pieces, chop fine a small piece of salt pork. Also chop fine four onions, then add salt and pepper, and cook all together until beans are tender.

Oil Dressing for Lettuce Salad (Mexican)

1 large onion, chopped fine
1 clove garlic, minced
2/3 cup sugar
2 tsp. prepared mustard
2/3 cup salad oil
1/3 cup vinegar
Paprika, several shakes
Salt and pepper to taste

Mix all ingredients well in a jar with lid and marinate a few hours in the refrigerator. Pour over wedges of crisp Iceberg lettuce.

"To make a perfect salad, there should be a spendthrift for oil, a miser for vinegar, a wise man for salt, and madcap to stir the ingredients up and mix them well together."
                                                        Old Spanish Proverb

Suculento (Mexican)

Fry 1/2 lb. chopped salt pork with a sliced onion and 6 green peppers cut small. When brown, add drained corn nibblets and 4 small summer squash, sliced. Cover with milk, and cook slowly, over low heat, two hours without stirring.

Corn was eaten in the old days as now in modern times. Usually it was roasted in its own husk in the ashes or coals of the fireplace. Sometimes the nibblets of green corn were cut off the ear and boiled with new beans. The Indians called it "Sukquitahash" or Succotash, as we know it today, when the corn is prepared with lima beans.

From Grits to Samp (Indian)

Early settlers livened up an Indian dish of hot grits (made from ground corn) by adding butter, milk, sugar, nutmeg and molasses or maple syrup. They then called the concoction "Samp".

Hills Bros.

Coffees,
Teas,
Spices,
Extracts

Strictly Pure and of the
Highest Grade

"Once Used, Always Used"

Beans in a Casserole (Spanish)

2 cups white or pink beans
1 onion, sliced
Small piece pork or bacon
1 cup canned tomatoes
2 shredded chili peppers
Tabasco sauce, to taste
Salt

Soak the beans overnight. In the morning, boil 15 minutes and drain. Fry the onion with the pork or bacon. Add these to the beans, also the tomatoes, peppers, Tabasco sauce, salt and sufficient hot water to cover well. Boil briskly for ten minutes, then put in a casserole and bake in a slow oven for four hours.

Mrs. Curtis' Cookbook

Linda Mazzuia's Gnocchi (Italian)

6 medium potatoes
3 eggs
1 pound flour (more or less as needed to
   to make dough firm and smooth)

Boil potatoes and put through potato ricer. Make a dough consisting of the riced potatoes, flour and eggs. Knead until smooth. Form into a roll, finger thin, and cut into pieces 1-1/2 inches long. Press each piece lightly with a fork. Place about 15 gnocchi in boiling, salted water. When they come to the surface, remove from water with strainer and place in a warm serving dish. Keep water boiling briskly, repeat until all gnocchi are cooked. Serve with salt, pepper and melted butter.

Josie Reece's Burnt Sugar Cake

1/2 cup sugar - burn in a heavy bottom pan until it smokes intensely and looks almost black.

Add 1/2 cup boiling water - boil together until it becomes a syrup, then set aside to cool.

Cream together:

> *1-1/2 cups sugar*
> *3/4 cup butter*
> *Yolks of 2 eggs (save whites)*

Add the burnt sugar mixture, then 1 cup of cold water or sour milk.

Sift 7 times:

> *3 cups of flour*
> *1 tsp. baking soda*

Put in half the flour mixture and beat. Add the second half and beat. Add 1 tsp. vanilla. Fold in the stiffly beaten whites of the two eggs. Bake in layer tins in a moderate oven (350 deg.)

Frosting for Josie Reece's Burnt Sugar Cake

2 cups sugar
1/2 cup butter
1/2 cup cream or milk
1 Tbsp. vanilla

> *Cook and beat until thick enough to frost cake.*

Hot Pot Irish Stew

2 pounds lamb suitable for stewing
2 pounds potatoes
3 carrots
4 onions
Salt, pepper, and a little flour
Water or stock

Cut the meat into pieces convenient for serving. Peel the potatoes and cut them into small, thick pieces; peel and slice the carrots diagonally; slice the onions thinly.

Mix the salt, pepper and flour and roll each piece of meat in the mixture. Put a layer of potatoes in a deep dish or wide-mouthed crock, then a layer of carrots, meat and onions. Repeat till the crock is full. Have potatoes for the last layer and fill the dish with water or stock. Bake three hours in a moderate oven, adding more liquid as necessary.

Serve in the crock, along with hot biscuits.

Wiener Schnitzel (German/Austrian)

2 pounds veal cutlets, cut into serving pieces and pounded very thin.

Chill the meat well and dip it into beaten egg and then in 1 part seasoned flour mixed with 3 parts fine dried bread crumbs. Let the breading dry for 1/2 hour.

Saute the cutlets slowly in butter until golden-brown.
Sprinkle with capers and serve with slices of lemon.

> **THE OXNARD**
>
> **UNDERTAKING**
>
> **COMPANY**
>
> are now in their new brick block, on the
> North Side of the Public Square,
> with
> large, beautiful funeral parlors,
> and a fine and complete line of stock
> always on hand.
> Special attention given to Picture Framing
>
> **CALL AND SEE US**

From the collection of Evelyn Lucille Reece.

A good portion of the early "Cookery Books", written in the 1800s and even after the turn of the century, included a section on preparing food for the infirm. Suffering from major illnesses and dying young, it seems, were not uncommon facts of life. Many children succumbed to such contagious diseases as typhoid and scarlet fevers, infantile paralysis, and influenza, with pneumonia probably the most common and dangerous complication. And, of course, untold numbers of women died in childbirth. Male and female, young and old, alike, fell victims to accidental death from dangerous backbreaking labor. Private family graveyards dotted the Santa Cruz Mountains.

Scotch Shortbread

1-1/2 cups flour
3/4 cup butter
1/2 cup sugar
1 oz. blanched almonds

Sift the flour twice and rub in the butter with the hands; add the sugar and knead and mix either on a board or in a bowl, till dough is formed. Do not add either egg or milk, as the butter softens with the mixing and will bind the ingredients together. Roll the dough rather thinly, cut into rounds or ovals and press a few almonds into each. Place on a flat baking pan, and bake in a slow oven till golden brown.

Boiled Coffee

2 level Tbsp. ground coffee
3 cups water
White of one egg

Grind the coffee moderately fine, add half the white of an egg to it and put into a perfectly clean coffee pot. Add enough cold water to moisten the coffee, then pour the measured water over, cover the pot closely and boil ten minutes. Then pour in half a cup of cold water, draw the pot to the side of the range and allow it to stand five minutes to settle before serving. Never let the coffee boil after the cold water has been added.

Hot Chocolate (Mexican)

2 squares semi-sweet chocolate
2 level tsp. sugar
4 Tbsp. water
3 cups milk
1 tsp. vanilla extract
Whipped cream
Dash of cinnamon

In a double boiler put the chocolate, sugar and water. Cook gently until the chocolate is melted. Add the milk gradually and bring to the boiling point. Beat until foamy, flavor with vanilla. Serve with a spoonful of whipped cream on top which has been dusted with a dash of cinnamon.

Mexican Flan

4 eggs, well beaten
1 cup milk
1 cup half-and-half (light cream)
1/4 cup sugar
2 tsp. vanilla
Brown sugar

Beat all ingredients except brown sugar, together until smooth. Pour into well-buttered 1-quart baking dish. Place dish in pan which has been filled with just enough hot water to come up around dish. Bake custard for 1 hour at 350 deg., or until knife inserted in center comes out clean. Chill for 3 - 4 hours then spread an even layer of light brown sugar over the top and broil 8" below flame until sugar is partially melted and lightly browned. Serve at once, with or without whipped cream.

Stuffed Baked Potatoes (Delicate and Different)

Scoop out center of baked potato, add a dash of California Sauterne. Beat to fluffiness.

Stuff back in shells.

French Lace Cookies

1   cup flour
1   cup finely chopped almonds
1/2 cup butter (1 cube)
2/3 cup brown sugar
1/2 cup light corn syrup

Combine flour and chopped nuts in mixing bowl. Melt butter, add brown sugar and syrup. Bring to a boil, stirring constantly. Add hot syrup mixture to flour and nuts. Stir until well mixed. Drop by 1/2 teaspoonful about 3" apart on oiled baking sheets. Bake at 325 deg. 8 - 10 minutes. Let Cool for a minute then remove with spatula.

Prune Whip

12 large prunes
 4 eggs
 1 cup of sugar
 pinch of salt
 1/2 tsp. cream of tartar

Cook the prunes until soft, remove the pits and chop fine. Beat the whites of the eggs to a very stiff froth and add the sugar and salt and cream of tartar. Fold in the chopped prunes. Mix all together.

Bake in a pudding pan set in hot water for 20 minutes.

Testimonials

A Bad Accident

Galena, Illinois
June 20, 1902

To: D. Ransom, Son and Company
     Buffalo, New York

Gentlemen:

About two years ago I had my hip broken, my knee twisted out of place, and my ankle twisted out of place, all at the same time. I tried various remedies without relief until by accident I learned of your "DERMADOR." I have used about $ 7.50 worth, and am able to walk about as well as I ever did, and am entirely free from pain and the rheumatism I had.

                    Yours truly,

                    (s) Captain William Fisher

* * *

Perry, Oklahoma
March 14, 1898

To: D. Ransom, Son and Company
     Buffalo, New York

Gentlemen:

I am in the Livery Business here. My teams have to be on the road for a week or so. When they come in, 9 out of every 10 have to be doctored. I use nothing but "DERMADOR."

                    Yours truly,

                    (s) Lacy - Eckles

* * *

Professor Anderson's "DERMADOR" consists of Alcohol 60% pure grain. Good for man or beast. (No *wonder* it was so popular!)

Sliced Tomato Salad Au Gratin

Cut a large ripe tomato in thick slices. Remove seedy portions.
Fill spaces left with Neufchatel Cheese moistened with cream.
Many artistic designs may be obtained in this way.
Serve garnished with lettuce.

Gendarme Potatoes

Peel even-sized potatoes and cut in eighths lengthwise.
Put in roasting pan with salt and a piece of butter.
Cook in hot oven seven minutes.
Add more butter, stir well, and cook until tender.
A simple way of making potatoes that look and taste French fried.

> From the Stanford University Hospital Cook Book
> through the courtesy of Victor Hirtzler
> Chef, St. Francis Hotel, San Francisco.

To Melt Butter, Which is Rarely Well done

Mix in the proportion of a teaspoon full of flour to four ounces
of the best butter on a trencher (carving board).
Put it into a small sauce pan, add two or three Tablespoonsful of
hot water, boil quick a minute, shaking it all the time
Milk used instead of water requires rather less butter and looks whiter.

Shallot Vinegar

Split 6 or 8 shallots.
Put them into a quart bottle, and fill it up with vinegar.
Stop it, and within a month it will be fit for use.

Coffee Ice Cream

Heat one pint strong left-over coffee, and add one-half pound sugar and stir until
dissolved; add two cans Borden's Evaporated Milk. Mix well and freeze.

The Story of Crisco
Circa 1911

"The culinary world is revising its entire cook book on account of the advent of Crisco, a new and altogether different cooking fat which is made from the oils of vegetables. (No other food supplies our bodies with the drive, the vigor, which fat gives.)

"Many wonder that any product could gain the favor of cooking experts so quickly. A few months after the first package was marketed, practically every grocery of the better class in the United States, was supplying women with the new product.

"This was largely because four classes of people - housewives, chefs, doctors, and dietitians - were glad to be shown a product which at once would make for more digestible foods, more economical foods, and better tasting foods."

* * *

The Story of Eagle Brand Condensed Milk

"In 1856, Mr. Gail Borden, after years of patient research, received from the United States Patent Office, the original patent for the Vacuum Process of Condensing and Preserving Milk. He then began the manufacture of such a product which he patriotically called the "Eagle Brand Condensed Milk", and it has since been universally regarded as the Standard of its kind. It is especially prepared with scrupulous care for use as an infant food but at the same time it meets all requirements for general use: for coffee, tea, chocolate, ice cream, puddings, sauces, and nearly all recipes calling for milk."

Harlequin Conserve

25 yellow peaches - wash, pare, and cut into small pieces
1 lb. white grapes - halve and seed
10 red plums - pare and cut into small pieces
1 pineapple - pare and cut into small pieces
1/4 lb. blanched almonds

Cook fruit together until soft and well blended.
Measure, allowing three-quarters of a cup of sugar for each cup of fruit.
Cook gently for 20 minutes, then add chopped almonds.
Cook for two hours or more, until thick and clear.
Put up in fancy fruit jars.

Left-Over Coffee

Even left-over coffee can be utilized.
Pour it off the grounds and set it away in the ice box.
When enough has been saved, make a coffee jelly or use in
a Mocha filling.

Corn Bread

1 cup cornmeal
2 Tbsp. melted Crisco
1 cup flour
1/2 cup sugar
1 cup sour cream
2 eggs
1/2 tsp. baking soda
1/2 tsp. salt

Mix cornmeal with flour, sugar, salt, Crisco, eggs well beaten, and baking soda mixed with cream.
Mix well and turn into Criscoed tin and bake in moderate oven 30 minutes.

The famous New England "Johnny Cake" consisted of cornmeal and milk baked hard so that it could be carried on long trips. A hungry traveler usually dipped it into cider or hot coffee to give it flavor and so that he could chew it.

Coffee Cake

2 cups brown sugar
1 cup butter
1 cup molasses
1 cup strong coffee
4 eggs beaten separately
1-1/2 tsp. baking soda
1-1/2 tsp. ground cloves
2 tsp. grated nutmeg
1 cup of raisins
1 cup currants
4 cups flour, sifted

Cream sugar and butter thoroughly.
Add molasses, eggs, baking soda, cloves, and nutmeg.
Alternately add the coffee and flour.
Stir in raisins and currants.
Put in greased cake pan and bake in moderate oven until done.

Scripture Cake

One cup butter	*Judges*	*5.25*
Three cups flour	*I. Kings*	*4.22*
Three cups sugar	*Jeremiah*	*6.20*
Two cups raisins	*I. Samuel*	*30.12*
One cup almonds	*Genesis*	*43.11*
One half cup water	*Genesis*	*24.17*
One half cup wine	*John*	*2. 9*
Six eggs	*Isaiah*	*10.14*
One tablespoon honey	*Genesis*	*43.11*
One teaspoon baking soda	*Leviticus*	*23.17*
Pinch of salt	*Leviticus*	*2.13*
Spice	*Genesis*	*43.11*

Follow Solomon's advice for
making good boys - i.e., beat well.

Food For Thought

A NEW SYSTEM OF DOMESTIC COOKERY, written by a Lady, and published in England in the year 1816, during difficult economic times, was discovered recently in Los Gatos, California. It originally sold for Seven Shillings and Sixpence in Boards (hard cover). There is no indication of original ownership, or how or when the book arrived in this area. It is not beyond reason, however, to assume it was one of the few and prized possessions of an early pioneering family. The text is preceded by the following advertisement:

"As the following directions were intended for the conduct of the families of the Authoress's own daughters, and for the arrangement of their table, so as to unite a good figure with proper economy, she has avoided all excessive luxury, such as essence of ham, and that wasteful expenditure of large quantities of meat for gravy, which so greatly contributes to keep up the price, and is no less injurious to those who eat, than to those whose penury obliges them to abstain. Many receipts are given for things which, being in daily use, the mode of preparing them may be supposed too well known to require a place in a cookery-book; yet we rarely meet with butter properly melted, good toast and water, or well made coffee. She makes no apology for minuteness in some articles, or for leaving others unnoticed, because she does not write for professional cooks. This little work would have been a treasure to herself when she first set out in life, and she therefore hopes it may prove useful to others. In that expectation it is given to the Public; and as she will receive from it no emolument, so she trusts it will escape without censure."

The authoress (who remains unnamed and uncompensated) had words of wisdom that continue to hold true in these more modern times:

"It is much to be feared, that for the waste of many of the good things that God has given for our use, not abuse, the mistress and servants of great houses will hereafter be called to a strict account.

"In some families, great loss is sustained by the spoiling of meat. If meat is brought from a distance in warm weather, the butcher should be ordered to cover it close, and bring it early in the morning; but even then, if it is kept on the road while he serves the customers who live nearest to him, it will very likely be fly-blown. Then those sections must be cut away and washed and scrubbed thoroughly. This happens often in the country.

"Observations Respecting Butter: There is no one article in family consumption more in use, of greater variety in goodness or that is of more consequence to have a superior quality than this, and the economizing of which is more necessary.

"It answers well to pay some boy employed in the farm or stable, so much a score for the eggs he brings in. It will be his interest then to save them from being purloined, which nobody but one in his situation can prevent. And sixpence or eight pence a score will be buying eggs cheap.

"For good butter keep the cows out of the turnips and cabbage patches as the resulting tastes can be very disagreeable.

"Vegetables soon sour and corrode metals and glazed red ware, by which a strong poison is produced. Some years ago, the death of several gentlemen was occasioned at Salt-Hill, by the cook sending a Ragout to the table which she had kept from the preceding day in a copper vessel badly tinned. Vinegar, by its acidity, does the same, the glazing being of lead or arsenic."

In her recipes the authoress reveals herself to be a good cook. She uses only the finest quality of real butter, milk, cream, herb s and spices, etc. For aromatic flavor enhancements she turns to salt, pepper (both black and white and cayenne), mace, nutmeg, cloves, mustard, vinegar, and interesting liquors and wines such as brandies, sherries and sweet ports.

Regarding her entrees, she also made use of the entire animal, fish or fowl being prepared, and included recipes for everything from ears and eyeballs to trotters and tails! There was very little wastage, if any. She even instructed on how to pluck and store feathers to be used later in the making of pillows and comforters.

Since it was, in those days, the woman's responsibility to take on the challenging and always intimidating art of carving, she included several illustrations of cuts of meat, poultry and game, and fish and how to tackle them properly. It distressed her that at a dinner party, for example, "Some hostesses haggle meat so much as not to be able to help half a dozen persons decently from a large tongue, or a sirloin of beef; and the dish goes away with the appearance of having been gnawed on by dogs!"

***

Very important was the introduction of the table fork. Its widespread acceptance in America, which took place by 1700, greatly changed habits of eating and entertaining. With the fork it was no longer desirable to have a piece of bone attached to each piece of meat for a handle. You could now also get rid of the dog waiting under the table for the bone!

And in closing:...

" There is no such thing as a little garlic."
Pathagoras

Household Discoveries

To clean coffee pots - Rub salt on the inside of a coffee pot to remove coffee and egg. Rinse quickly and thoroughly.

The optimum laundry closet involved far more chemistry in the old days containing such items as chemical soaps, Oxalic Acid, Citric Acid, Tartaric Acid, Muriatic Acid, Salts of Lemon, Ammonia, Alcohol, Chloroform, Turpentine, Chlorine, Bleaching Powders, and even a supply of Gasoline!

When hanging up clothes in freezing weather it is suggested: Set the clothespin bag in a kettle of boiling water. Remove and dry near the stove. The hot clothes-pins will help keep the hands warm when it's cold outside.

Half the disagreeableness of house cleaning is taken away by having a lotion to apply to parboiled and uncomfortable hands. Soak 2 or 3 ounces of Quince Seed overnight, strain through cheese cloth, and add 2 quarts of water and 2 ounces each of Glycerin, Boric Acid, and Witch Hazel. This is one of the best of lotions.

At one point in directions for making a sizing solution (starch) with isinglass shavings, it says "Cork the bottle to prevent evaporation, but not tightly enough to cause explosion." - A fine line.

Household Remedies

To Prevent Sleeplessness - Take a warm bath just before retiring. Or wet a cloth in cold water and lay it on the back of the neck. Or rub the body gently with a flesh brush for ten or fifteen minutes. Or drink a cup of hot milk on retiring, or a glass of buttermilk. Or drink a tumblerful of water containing a teaspoonful of Magnesia and a few drops of Aqua Ammonia or Sal Volatile.

For Indigestion: A teaspoon of glycerine in a little water taken after each meal is a good remedy.

To Remove Warts: Castor oil applied to warts regularly at night for a while will dry them up.

A Tired Brain: Horsford's Acid Phosphate acts as a tonic, increasing the capacity for mental labor, relieving the tired brain, and imparting new energy to that organ.

In the top 1904 photograph, courtesy of William A. Wulf, the tracks of the San Jose-Los Gatos Interurban Railway are visible in the dirt street in front of the gracious Lyndon Hotel located at the corner of Santa Cruz Avenue and Main Street. The newly installed power distribution poles are plainly in view. The bottom photo, looking west, shows a more mature Lyndon Hotel at the height of its career in the mid-fifties before it was sadly torn down (in 1963) in the name of progress. The only remaining evidence of the hotel today are the Palm trees which were left standing. From the Jensen collection.

BIBLIOGRAPHY - Part 1
History

Baggerly, John. "Rowdies, Romance, Death Rode the Interurban."
Los Gatos, California: Los Gatos-Saratoga Times Observer, April 2, 1985, p. 3.

Barnacle, Betty. "Walking in the Moccasins of the Costanoan."
San Jose, California: San Jose News, March 15, 1977, p. 6A.

Bennett, Mardi. "French Reminiscences."
San Jose, California: San Jose Mercury News, February 10, 1988, Extra 3.

A BRIEF HISTORY OF WELLS FARGO.
San Francisco, Calif.: Wells Fargo Bank, c. 1971.

Browne, J. Ross. ILLUSTRATED NARRATIVE OF THE FAR WEST

Bruntz, George C. THE HISTORY OF LOS GATOS.
Fresno, California: Valley Publishers, c. 1971, 173 pp.

Brusa, Betty War. SALINAN INDIANS OF CALIFORNIA AND THEIR NEIGHBORS.
Healdsburg, California: Naturegraph Publishers, Inc., c. 1975, 97 pp.

Cohen, Susan. "Quake-Shaken Caruso Finally Wins Forgiveness."
San Jose, California: San Jose News, April 17, 1980.

Colgrove, George Lewis. "The Life Story of George L. Colgrove, Pioneer Californian, Stage Driver and Railroad Man, as Told by Himself." Edited by George C. Hildebrand, 1974. From the William A. Wulf Collection.

Earl, Phillip. "Miners, Labor Unions Fought Hiring of Chinese Workers."
Reno, Nevada: Reno Gazette-Journal, January 24-30, 1994, p. 3.

Erdoes, Richard. SALOONS OF THE OLD WEST.
New York, N.Y.: Alfred A. Knopf, c. 1979, p. 183.

Florin, Lambert. GHOST TOWNS OF THE WEST.
New York, N.Y.: Promontory Press, c. 1971, p. 239.

Fox, Frances L. RINCONADA DE LOS GATOS.
Brown & Kauffmann, Inc., c. 1968.

Halle, Frederick. HISTORY OF SAN JOSE AND SURROUNDINGS WITH BIOGRAPHICAL SKETCHES OF EARLY SETTLERS. San Francisco, California: Bancroft Printer, 1871, pp. 193-194.

Harden, Grant. "Saint Clare Church Marks 200th Year." San Jose, California: Sunday Mercury News, April 10, 1977, pp. 33-34.

Hassrick, Royal B. THE COLORFUL STORY OF THE AMERICAN WEST. London, England: Octopus Books Ltd., c. 1975, 128 pp.

Heizer, Robert F. THE COSTANOAN INDIANS. Cupertino, California: De Anza College, c. 1974, 113 pp.

Heizer, Robert F. LANGUAGES, TERRITORIES AND NAMES OF CALIFORNIA INDIAN TRIBES. Berkeley, California: University of California Press, c. 1966, 62 pp.

Horan, James D. THE AUTHENTIC WILD WEST: THE OUTLAWS. New York: Crown Publishers, Inc., c. 1977, pp. 167-202.

Iacopi, Robert. EARTHQUAKE COUNTRY. Menlo Park, California: Lane Magazine and Book Company, c. 1971, 160 pp.

Koch, Margaret. SANTA CRUZ COUNTY, PARADE OF THE PAST. Fresno, California: Valley Publishers, c. 1973, 254 pp.

Koch, Margaret. THEY CALLED IT HOME, SANTA CRUZ, CALIFORNIA. Fresno, California: Valley Publishers, c. 1974.

Loomis, Patricia. "Gala Celebrations Planned as San Jose Nears 200th Birthday." San Jose, California: Sunday Mercury News, January 30, 1977, p. 1 Vantage '77.

Loomis, Patricia. "The Little Man who Saved San Francisco." (Brig. Gen. Frederick Funston.) San Jose, California: San Jose News, April 18, 1980, p. B1.

MacGregor, Bruce A. SOUTH PACIFIC COAST. Berkeley, California: Howell-North Books, c. 1968.

McCarthy, Lea F. THE GUNFIGHTERS. Berkeley, California: Mike Roberts Color Productions, c. 1959, 44 pp.

McLoughlin, Denis. WILD & WOOLLY - An Encyclopedia of the Old West. Garden City, New York: DoubleDay & Co., Inc., c. 1975.

Martin, Edward. HISTORY OF SANTA CLARA COUNTY.
Los Angeles, California: Historic Record Co., 1911.

"Nostalgia", CALIFORNIA TODAY: San Jose, California: San Jose Mercury News Sunday Magazine, Oct. 2, 1977.

"The Old Explorer". NATIONAL GEOGRAPHIC SCHOOL BULLETIN. November 8, 1971, No. 9, p. 142.

Oman, Anne H. "Indian Corn Helped Build a Hemisphere". NATIONAL GEOGRAPHIC SCHOOL BULLETIN. February 4, 1974, No. 19, pp. 300-301.

Opie, Iona and Peter. CHILDREN'S GAMES IN STREET AND PLAYGROUND. Great Britain: Oxford University Press, c. 1969, pp. 149-183.

Payne, Stephen. A HOWLING WILDERNESS. Santa Cruz, California: Loma Prieta Publishing Co., c. 1978, 159 pp.

Rambo, F. Ralph. REMEMBER WHEN. San Jose, California: Rosicrucian Press, c. 1965.

Roske, Ralph J. EVERYMAN'S EDEN - A HISTORY OF CALIFORNIA. New York, N.Y.: The MacMillan Co., c. 1968.

Schreibman, Jack. "Russians Sought More Than Otter Pelts in California." San Jose, California: San Jose News, May 10, 1977, p. 7AW.

"Sense of the Seventies - California 100 Years Ago".
Burlingame, California: California Historical Society, c. 1970.

Smith, Verla Lee. "Mission Bells Echo California Past". NATIONAL GEOGRAPHIC SCHOOL BULLETIN. November 17, 1969, No. 10, pp. 152-155.

Spearman, Arthur Dunning. THE FIVE FRANCISCAN CHURCHES OF MISSION SANTA CLARA. Palo Alto, California: The National Press, c. 1963, p. 19.

Stanger, Frank M. SOUTH FROM SAN FRANCISCO.
San Mateo, California: The San Mateo County Historical Association, c. 1963.

Stell, Jose. "Naming Santa Cruz Mountain Pass A Frustrating Task." San Jose, California: San Jose News, March 15, 1977, p. 1BW.

Strobel, Bill. "Ruin, Ruin, Ruin - This Was S.F. 72 Years Ago." San Jose, California: San Jose News, April 18, 1978, p. B1.

Tabari, Pam. "Ida Berti Cavallini." Los Gatos, California: Los Gatos Times, 1984.

Wagner, Jack R.
 THE LAST WHISTLE.

Watkins, T. H. CALIFORNIA AN ILLUSTRATED HISTORY.
 New York: American Legacy Press, c. 1983, pp. 35-40.

WATSONVILLE - THE FIRST HUNDRED YEARS. Watsonville, California:
 Watsonville Chamber of Commerce, c. 1952, p. 80.

"Ways With Wine." Compiled and edited by Paul Masson's.
 Saratoga, California: Paul Masson Vineyards, c. 1968, 29 pp.

Wulf, William A. "Los Gatos Landmark Observes Anniversary." (Historic Toll House.)
 Los Gatos, California: Los Gatos - Saratoga Times Observer, November 15, 1977, p. 1.

Yellow Bird (John Rollin Ridge). THE LIFE AND ADVENTURES OF JOAQUIN
 MURIETA. Norman, Oklahoma: University of Oklahoma Press, c. 1955, p. 159.

Young, John V. GHOST TOWNS OF THE SANTA CRUZ MOUNTAINS.
 Santa Cruz, California: Western Tanager Press, c. 1984, 194 pp.

BIBLIOGRAPHY - Part 2
Food and Recipes

Adamson, Helen Lyon. GRANDMOTHER IN THE KITCHEN. New York, N.Y.: Crown Publishers, Inc., c. 1965.

Allen, Ida C. Bailey. MRS. ALLEN'S COOKBOOK.
Boston, Mass.: Small, Maynard & Co. Publishers, c. 1917.

BORDEN'S RECIPES.
New York, N.Y.: Borden's Condensed Milk Company (Est. 1857), 25pp.

Butel, Jane. HOTTER THAN HELL. Los Angeles, California: HPBooks, A Division of Price Stern Sloan, Inc., c. 1987, 199 pp.

Calvello, Tony, Bruce Harlow, Georgia Sackett, Shirley Sarvis. SAN FRANCISCO FIRE HOUSE FAVORITES. New York, N.Y.: Bobbs-Merrill Co., Inc., c. 1965.

COLLECTION OF RECIPES USED IN STANFORD UNIVERSITY HOSPITAL.
Palo Alto, Ca.: Stanford University Press, 40 pp.

THE FIRESIDE CALENDAR & ENGAGEMENT BOOK.
New York, N.Y.: Simon & Schuster, c. 1960.

Harris, Gertrude. FOODS OF THE FRONTIER.
San Francisco, California: 101 Productions, c. 1972, 192 pp.

Harrison, Grace Clergue and Gertrude Clergue. ALLIED COOKERY (British, Belgian, French, Italian, Russian) To Aid the War Sufferers of the Devastated Districts of France. New York, N.Y.: G. P. Putnam's Sons. c. 1916, 108 pp.

Mansur, Caroline E. (Compiler). THE VIRGINIA HOSTESS, SEVENTEENTH AND EIGHTEENTH CENTURY, VOL. I. U.S.: Judd and Detweiler, Inc., c. 1960, 102 pp.

Morse, Sidney. HOUSEHOLD DISCOVERIES, AN ENCYCLOPEDIA OF PRACTICAL RECIPES AND PROCESSES. San Jose, Calif.: The Success Co., 1908.

A NEW SYSTEM OF DOMESTIC COOKERY. Adapted to the use of private families. By a Lady. London: Caledonian Mercury Press, Pub. 1816, 354 pp.

ORIGINAL MEXICANS, The. Hartford, Connecticut: Heublein, Inc., c. 1972.

Morse, Sidney.
HOUSEHOLD DISCOVERIES - AN ENCYCLOPEDIA OF PRACTICAL RECIPES AND PROCESSES.
San Jose, California: The Success Co., 1908.

A NEW SYSTEM OF DOMESTIC COOKERY. Adapted to the use of private families. By a Lady.
London: Caledonian Mercury Press, Pub. 1816, 354 pp.

ORIGINAL MEXICANS, The.
Hartford, Connecticut: Heublein, Inc., c. 1972.

Paul, Virginia (Editor).
THE HOMESTEAD COOKBOOK.
Seattle Washington: Superior Publishing Co., c. 1976, 127 pp.

PLEASANT VALLEY COOKBOOK.
Pleasant Valley, California: circa 1920.

RECIPES, AMERICAN COOKING: THE GREAT WEST.
Foods of the World, Time-Life Series, N.Y., c. 1971.

STORY OF CRISCO, THE.
Cincinnati, Ohio: Proctor & Gamble Co., c 1913, 231pp.

Wallace, Lily Haxworth.
THE RUMFORD COMPLETE COOK BOOK.
Rhode Island: The Rumford Chemical Works, c. 1930, 236 pp.

INDEX

Adams' Grove 97, 110
Adams, Delia Roxana Cooper 96, 98, 105, 106, 117
Adams, Edward F. 95-98, 106, 182
Adams, Katherine 122
Adams, Ned 116
Agricultural Works 176
Alameda 69, 81, 141, 175
Allen, Charles H. 95
Alma 63, 71, 77, 144, 176, 184, 188-189
Alma Station 84
Alvarado, Juan 17
Austrian Gulch 95
Aztec Indian 8-9

Bascom, "Grandma" 53, 191
Beehive ix, x
Belden, Josiah 21
Bell, Doctor 40
Benicia 29
Berricke, Barbara 38, 39
Bidwell-Bartelson 17
Big Basin State Park 98
Big Red 159, 161
Big Trees 82
Black Bart aka: Charles Bolton 65
Bliss, Mrs. 100
Bonanza King 92
Boulder Creek 43, 141, 143, 147
Branham, Isaac 21, 33, 34
Broad Gauge Railroad 141, 143, 145, 154
Burrell, Birney 34
Burrell, Clarissa 34, 35
Burrell, Lyman 34, 37, 41, 95, 105

California State Highway 5 184
California State Highway 9 51
California State Highway 17 3, 170, 176, 184

California, State of
  Act of Removal 29
  Angel's Camp 25
  Bear Flag 20
  Bridgeport 17
  Constitution 29
  Convention, Monterey 29
  Markleeville 17
  San Jose, First Capitol 29
  Sierra Range 17
California-Nevada Gold Rush
  Aurora 26
  Bodie 26
  French Gulch 25
  Sutter's Creek 24
  Virginia City 26
Cameron, Donaldina 145
Candlestick Park 185
Carson, Kit (Christopher) 17-18
Caruso, Enrico 175, 177, 178
Carver, Hannah 49
Castle, O. B. 78
Castro, General Jose 17-20
Cat's Canyon 1, 143, 149, 151
Catala, Father 9
Chamberlain, Will 105, 116
Chase's Lumber Mill 110
Chinese 49, 51, 53, 71-72, 81, 145, 146, 175
Cinnabar 5
Civil War 69, 117
Clough, Delford 100, 101, 105
Clough, Mr. and Mrs. 100-101, 105
Colgrove, George L. 56-60, 63-64, 77, 81-82, 105, 153, 182-184
Commonwealth Club of California 97
Comstock Mine 26
Comstock, Henry "Pancake" 26
Concord Coach 56, 58, 68
Congress Springs 170-171, 172

Consolidated Virginia Mine 69
Cook, Mrs. 77
Cortez, Hernando 45
Cosmopolitan Hotel 133
Crall, George 187
Crane (later Rapp) Ranch 114, 136
Croquet 122, 126
Creeks
  Bean 49, 64
  Bear 51, 184-185
  Black x, 51, 184-185
  Guadalupe 7-8
  King's 59
  Little Deer 176
  Los Gatos 1, 18, 22-23, 31-33, 49, 51, 64, 144-145, 152, 163, 170, 176
  Saratoga 171
  Stevens Creek 9
  Zayante 43

Davidson, Peter 51
Davis, Alfred E. "Hog" 69-70, 77, 81-82
Davis, Thomas 70, 71
de Anza, Jean Bautista 13
de Cuervo, Jose 13
de Havilland, Olivia 172
de la Pena, Father 7
de Lausen, Fermin Francisco 8
de Neve, Don Felipe 8
de Romeau, San Jose Antonio 8
Delmas, Delphin 98
Donner Party 21
Dye, Job 43

Earthquake/Fire of 1906/1989 86, 88, 132, 158, 163, 175-179, 183, 185
El Camino Real 7, 10, 32
Espediente and Diseno 11, 32
Eva 176

Fair, James G. 69-70, 144
Farnham, Eliza W. (Mrs.) 25, 50
Felton, Town of 43, 70, 77, 81, 143-144
Ferguson Brothers 59-60
First Train to Santa Cruz 187
Fisher, Captain William 18
Flag-Raising Ceremony 103, 123
Fontaine, Joan 172
Fontaine, Lilian 172
Forbes' Mill 22, 44
Forbes, Alexander 22, 24
Forbes, James Alexander 22, 23
Forest House 77
Fort Ross 19
Franciscan Trail ix, 8, 33, 49, 51
Franciscans, Order of 7, 9, 33
Fremont, Captain John C. 17-20
French Settlers 133
Funston, Brig. Gen. Frederick 177-178

Gabilan Mountains 5, 18
Gage, Governor Henry T. 98
Galindo, Maria Ana 22
Galindo, Juan Christomo 22
Garcia 147
Garcia, Manuel 27-28, 105
Garrod, Emma Stolte 149-151
German Settlers 133, 145
Gilroy, John 21
Glenwood Hotel 83, 91-92
Glenwood Park 83
Glenwood Station 89
Glenwood, Town of 49, 61, 77-78, 81, 83, 86-93, 98, 104, 141, 176

Hamilton, Albert P. 63-65, 105
Hanks, Isabella 21
Hanks, Willard M. "Julian" 21, 29, 33-34, 105

Hartwell, Edward Petty 18
Hawk's Peak 18
Henning, John Pennell 52
Hernandez, Jose 32
Highland Grange 97, 110
Highland Grange Summer School 97, 110
Highland School District 99-101
Highland, M. C. 72
Highland/Skyland 75, 105, 119, 135, 138
Hihn, Frederic A. 70, 86
Hill, Andrew P. 38, 98
Hoffman's Shingle Mill 176
Hollister 61-62
Holy City 184
Hotel de Redwood 83, 88
Hotel Glen Orchy 83, 93
Hume, James B. 65

Indians
　Aptos 3
　Costanoan (Ohlone) 3-5, 10
　Pico, Marcelo 8-10
　Soquel 3
　Sun God's Sanctuary 9
　Superstitions 6
　Umunhum 3
　Weapons 4
　Yoscolo, the Renegade 8
　Zayante 3
Ingersoll, Doctor 40
Interurban Railway 157-158, 160-161, 170, 172

Jesuits 7, 46
Johnson, Joseph 51
Jones, Zachariah "Buffalo" 33-34, 49-52, 105

Jose, Don 18-19

Kennedy, James 52
Knowles, Dr. Frank 164
Koch, Margaret 49

La Porte, Earl 87
La Rinconada de Los Gatos 32
Lake Lexington (Reservoir) 84, 184, 189
Laguna Seca 18
Laurel 51, 61, 99, 104-105, 124, 143, 175, 176
LeFranc and Masson 46
LeFranc, Charles 46, 95
Lexington 21, 33-34, 43, 51-52, 57-58, 77, 84, 105, 184
Loma Prieta 96, 98, 176, 185
London, Jack 172
Los Angeles 19, 45, 62, 69
Los Gatos Mail Newspaper 141, 144
Los Gatos Schools 168-169, 172-173
Los Gatos, Town of 1, 5, 9, 23-24, 31-33, 43, 46, 52, 57, 61, 69, 71, 77, 83, 89, 143-174, 175, 177, 185
Love, Captain Harry 28, 37

Macabee Gopher Trap 173
Magnetic Springs 83, 94
Main Street Bridge, Los Gatos 52, 147, 155, 158, 170
Main, Mary 184-185
Mare Vista 95
Martin, Charles 49-50, 59, 78, 83, 89-91, 98, 105
Martin, Madame Zulema 95
Masson, Paul 46, 95
Matanza 11
McCracken, Josephine Clifford 74, 79, 98, 101, 105, 173

McKiernan, Charles Henry ix, 37-41, 44, 49-50, 58-59, 64-65, 89, 98, 105, 183
Micheltorena, General 17
Miller, Anson S. 99
Miller, George 99
Miller, Laurea 122
Miller, Milton 99
Ming Quong 145
Missions of California
  List of Missions 10
  San Carlos 8
  San Jose de Guadalupe 10
  Santa Clara 8-9, 22, 31-32
  Santa Cruz 8, 32
  Secularization 9
Mitchel, Reverend 104, 127
Mole' 14
Monterey 1, 11, 18, 20, 29, 37
Montezuma School 172
Moody's Gulch 57, 71, 177
Moody, D. B. 52
Moraga, Lt. Jose Joaquin 7
Morris, Theodore J. 170
Mother Lode 25-26, 49-61
Mount Shasta 19
Mountain Charley Tree x, 98
Murphy, John 50
Murrietta, Joaquin 27-28, 61, 105

Narrow Gauge Rail System 44, 69, 70 77, 81, 141, 143-144, 152, 154, 176
Nevada, State of
  Aurora 26
  Comstock Mine 26
  Consolidated Virginia Mine 69
  East Walker River 17
  High Sierra 25
  Mason Valley 17

Miners' Union 51
  Tybo 51
New Almaden 5, 8, 18, 22, 43
Nippon Mura 170
Norton, H. B. 95, 105, 115

Oakland 69, 143, 149, 175, 177-178, 183
Ohlone 15
Old San Jose Road 88
Opera Houses
  Ford, Los Gatos 158
  Johnson, Los Gatos 158
  Seanor, Los Gatos 158, 167
  Summit, Santa Cruz Mountains 104, 128
Ortega, Jose 13
Ortega, Emile 13
Orton, Bob 63

Pacific Ocean House 68
Panama-Pacific Intn'l Exposition 132, 183
Parkhurst, Charley 67
Parks Bill 98
Patchen 59, 63, 64
Paturot, Jerome 33
Peralta, Sebastian 32
Perkins, Governor George C. 96
Phelan, Senator James D. 172
Phylloxera 197
Pico, Marcelo 8-10
Pico, Governor Pio 19-20
Pioneer Stage Line 57-59
Plank and Turnpike Road Act 50-52
Pulque 54-55

Quito Trail 9

Rankin, Dora 147-149, 172, 177
Redwood District 52, 147
Richards, John E. 98
Richter Scale 175-181
Roads
  Bear Creek 51
  Glenwood Highway 51
  Laurel 51
  Old San Jose Road 88
  Saratoga and Pescadero Tpk 51
  Soquel 51
  Summit 51
  The Alameda 8

Sacramento 29, 69
Sacred Heart Novitiate 46
Sal, Hermenegildo (Don) 8
San Andreas Fault Line 2, 30, 185
San Diego, City of 7, 10
San Francisco Bay 1, 3, 7, 10, 13, 29, 61, 69, 97, 132, 175
San Francisco Chronicle 97
San Francisco City Hall 69, 179
San Francisco, City of 3, 7-8, 10, 13, 19, 22-23, 25-26, 50, 65, 69, 73, 77, 81, 84, 86, 96-98, 132-133, 145, 149, 175-181
San Gabriel 45
San Jose, City of 8, 10, 11, 15, 17-21 25-27, 29-30, 32-33, 38, 40, 43, 50, 53, 57-63, 69, 73, 81, 95, 98, 144, 147, 158, 160, 163-164, 170, 172, 175, 178
San Jose Census 15
San Lorenzo River 1, 43, 60
San Mateo Locomotive 73
San Quentin 65
Santa Clara Co. Fruit Exchange 96
Santa Clara Valley 1, 3, 7, 11, 18, 22, 25, 27, 32, 37, 43, 45, 59, 95, 98, 172

Santa Clara/Santa Cruz County 61-62
Santa Clara/Santa Cruz County Line ix, 30, 50, 51, 150-151
Santa Cruz & Felton RR 70-77
Santa Cruz Gap Turnpike JSC 50-52
Santa Cruz Mountains
1, 3, 4, 8, 15, 18, 21, 33, 37, 39, 41, 46, 49, 51, 57-59, 61, 63, 65, 67-69, 75, 81, 95, 97-98, 104, 107, 112, 118, 136-138, 140, 143-145, 149
Santa Cruz Sentinel Newspaper 98
Santa Cruz Stage Company 58, 68
Santa Cruz, Town of
8, 10, 18, 30-33, 393, 41, 43-44, 49-50, 56-60, 62-63, 68-69, 70, 77, 81-82, 89, 98-99, 137, 141, 148, 151-152, 173, 177, 185
Santa Rosa, Town of 175
Santa Rosa Brand Flour Mill 23-24
Saratoga, Town of
46, 51, 59, 64, 93, 148, 157, 163, 167, 170-172, 176
School Districts - Santa Cruz Mts.
99-101, 103, 122, 126
Schultheis, John and Susan 41, 61, 99, 104-105
Sempervirens Club 98
Serbrian, Gabriel 32
Serra, Father Junipero 7-8, 45
Shuford, J. C. 87
Sidneyites 61
Skipp, Miriam 102
Skyland Presbyterian Church 104, 127
Skyline Road 149-151
Slaughter's Lagoon 111
Slaughter, Colonel 100, 101, 105, 111, 112
Sloat, John Drake 20
Smith, John Pursly 63

Smith, Joseph 57
Smythe, George B. 65, 105
Soquel, Town of 59, 67, 88
South Pacific Coast Railroad Company
70, 71, 77, 84, 85, 144, 153
Southern Pacific RR 84, 143, 144,
153, 170
Spalsbury, E. 99
Spalsbury, Mrs. S. H. 99
Sporting Events 15
Stage Coach Toll Stations 49-52
Stanford, Leland 144
Stanford University 97, 176, 181
Steinbeck, John 172
Stevens Creek 9
Stowell, Levi 33
Summer Home Farm 83
Summit Blacksmith Shop 95, 176
Summit Social Club 104
Sunset Park 83, 85, 143, 184
Swain Brothers 57
Swift 60

Taylor, John 37, 40
Thee, Etienne 46, 95
Tomlinson, Ambrose 43
Touchard, Gustave 23
Tunnel Saloon 74, 78
Tunnel System
71-72, 74-75, 77-79, 86-87, 141,
143, 144-145, 176, 183
Twain, Mark 173

U.S. Land Commission 30
University of California 97

Vallejo, Town of 29
Vallejo, General Mariano 17, 20
Vasona 5
Vasquez, Tiburcio 61-62, 105
Vermilion Wars 5
Vignes, Jean Louis 45
Villa Branciforte 41
Villa Fontenay 83
Villa Montalvo 172

Ward and Colgrove 57, 63
Water Flume 144, 151-152
Watsonville 67, 70, 141
Webster, Daniel (Quote) 186
Wells Fargo History 26, 56, 65
Wells, Harry G. 98
Wine 45-47
Wright, James R. 85, 105
Wrights, Town of
34, 63-64, 71, 74, 77-79, 81, 83, 85-86,
99, 104, 141, 143-144, 175-176, 183
Wrights Presbyterian Church 104

Yocco, Ella Knowles 164
Young, Walter 57
Young, William A. 104, 105, 110, 119

Addendum Index
Hihn Sawmill 42
Jones, Billy   234
Lyndon Hotel 216
Sears Ranch Hazelhurst 48, 229, 230, 231
Sears, Rev. A. E.   103
Sears, William 48, 230
Willows Resort   82
Wilson's Market   231

Photo Addendum

Through the courtesy of historian William A. Wulf, the following photographs and memorabilia are included to enhance the knowledge of the Santa Cruz Mountain area at the turn of the last century. Thanks also to mountain residents David Rapp, Patsy Rapp, Emma Mae (Rapp) Lydon, Barbara Taylor, Margaret Burdett, Phil Mason, Marlene Wiley, M'Jeanne Erwin, Charlotte Piva, and Terry Maggi for helping to "fill in the gaps" for the second edition.

This overview photograph of the Sears Ranch shows the main residence, water tank house, barn, various other outbuildings and the well-established cherry and plum orchards in bloom circa 1910. The ranch was called "Hazelhurst," and was located on the Soquel-San Jose Road at the intersection of Morrell Cut Off, in the area now occupied by the many homes of Summit Woods. The two strangely tall trees shown in the background of the ranch look like giant bottle brushes. Many of the early settlers groomed and trimmed their Redwoods for various reasons, as Redwoods have a tendency to dominate the area around them.

The photograph above shows the well designed and beautifully maintained Sears Ranch facing on Soquel-San Jose Road. The lower photograph indicates it's cherry picking time again. Two horses are shown pulling a sled filled with packing crates. If the lady shown is Mrs. Sears, she is probably contemplating the baking of a lot of cherry pies.

The top photograph shows a four-horse-drawn wagon from Wilson's Market of Los Gatos making a delivery to the Sears' Ranch in a rare snow storm in the Santa Cruz Mountains. It was a 25-mile round-trip! Below is shown a horse-drawn Fresno Road Scraper being used to grade the road near the Sears' Ranch. It took two men and four horses to properly operate the grader. There was also probably a water tank somewhere nearby to quell the dust.

The upper photograph shows the Southern Pacific Railroad's Engine No. 1373 on the Sunset Park spur at Wrights, California, about 1909. The little boy dressed up like a conductor and the little girl for a Sunday picnic, are probably the children of the crew. The bottom photograph shows the Southern Pacific Railroad train at Mount Herman, circa 1915. This was the popular religious retreat not far from Felton, and everyone was dressed appropriately.

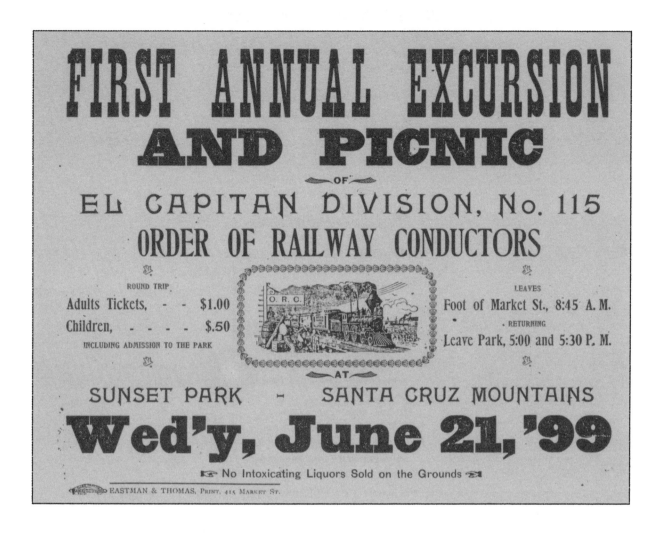

The El Capitan Division of the Order of Railway Conductors had their first annual excursion and picnic outing in 1899 at Sunset Park not far from the Wrights Station. The trip started in San Francisco at 8:45 A.M. and returned in the evening at 5:00 P.M. The round trip price of adult tickets, which included admission to the park, was only $1.00 and a mere 50 cents for children. The flyer indicated "No Intoxicating Liquors Sold on the Grounds."

THE MAN WITH THE OVERALLS
An Anonymous Poem   March 24, 1906
From the Billy Jones Collection of Railroad Memorabilia
Courtesy of William A. Wulf

Jake Kenney, with his section crew
Of twenty men so strong,
Went up the S.P. narrow gauge
To fix what had gone wrong.

A mile this side of Glenwood
Two hundred feet of track,
Owing to the heavy rain,
Had weakened in the back.

It did not take Jake Kenney long
Two hundred feet to brace,
Without a single cuss or swear
Or frown upon his face.

He gave his orders quick and firm
And his able force obeyed,
So soon the sunken track was fixed,
And O'Neil was not delayed.

He only spoke one language,
This section boss of fame,
But his crew they understood him
And got there just the same.

Said Eastern tourist on the train,
The like was never beat,
To see an Irish section boss
Not curse, it was a treat.

Conductor Tom just winked and smiled
For well indeed he knew,
That section men like Kenney
On the S.P. force were few.

At nine the train reached Laurel
To learn that farther on,
Another slide had taken place
For them to work upon.

There, with united effort
Of a crew from San Jose
They fixed a far more dangerous place,
And the train went on its way.

So life upon the narrow gauge
Has oft its ups and falls,
But the men who do the leading stunts
Are the men in the overalls.

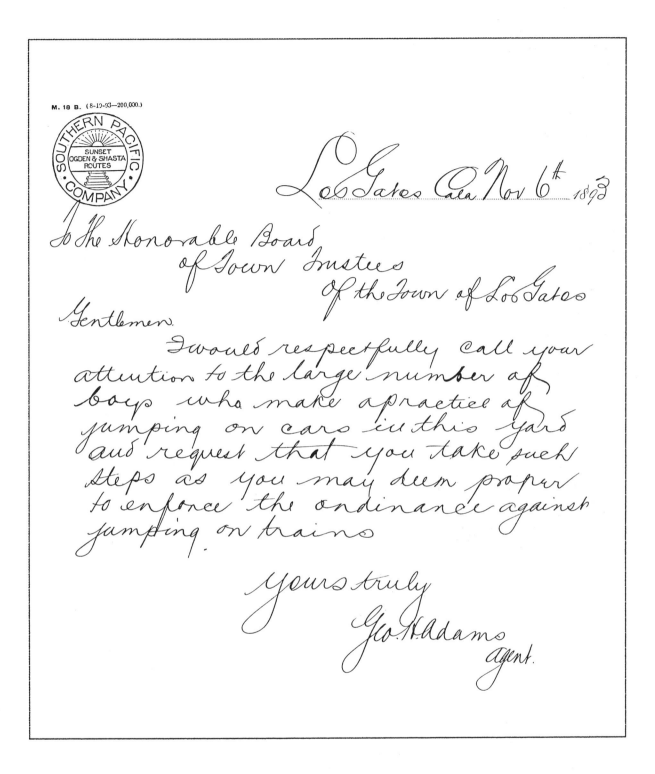

In addition to the problem of children taking short cuts through the railroad's mountain tunnels, which was, needless to say, a very dangerous thing to do, here was described another problem, that of boys jumping on the trains in the Los Gatos yards. George H. Adams, Agent for the S.P. Company in Los Gatos, wrote a letter to the Board of Trustees of the Town in 1893, requesting that the ordinance against such mischief be enforced.

ABOUT THE AUTHORS

My husband and I moved to the Glenwood area of the Santa Cruz Mountains in 1957, the year after we were married. On the 20 beautiful acres we purchased, we first developed a site for our 40-foot house trailer and a spring that supplied us with orange but ample mountain water. Six years later, we widened and deepened that original site to accommodate a home we designed and built ourselves. As we poured the concrete foundation, news of a child's impending arrival into this world demanded we increase the number of bedrooms by one. Our son grew up here for the first 6 years of his life, and also has wonderful recollections of our mountain home.

A portion of the "Old Glenwood Highway" and Bean Creek formed the southwestern border of the property, which was, no doubt, part of Charley McKiernan's land holdings 100 years before. When we came here, the old Glenwood one-room school house was still standing just down the road, there were remnants of a shake and shingle mill up one of our canyons, Mt. Charley's Tree was within a stone's throw of us in one direction, the portal to the Glenwood-Laurel Tunnel in another; and the infamous San Andreas Fault was a mile or so to the north as the crow flies.

Fascinated with the mystery, beauty, the dangers, and the history all around us, we began our research for this book.

For several years we both also worked in the rapidly expanding Aerospace Industry, in the Bay Area's Silicon Valley. I took a several year respite when we had our child but went back into business in Los Gatos in 1978 when we bought an existing store and I became sole proprietor.

In 1991, a year-and-a-half after the Loma Prieta Earthquake which greatly affected our area, we began to think of retirement. And, at the end of that year, we moved to Gardnerville, Nevada where we now make our home. The view from our large dining room window takes in the "backside" of the High Sierra as it enfolds Lake Tahoe. We never tire of this panorama, and we were inspired and determined in 1994 to finish our original manuscript on the Santa Cruz Mountains of California started so many years ago. Public acceptance of the Collectors Edition has been gratifying and on-going. One thing about history, it never gets old - only older - hence this Second Revised Edition.

Billie J. and Reece C. Jensen